Student Support Materials for **AQA**

A2 Biology

Unit 5: Control in Cells and in Organisms

Author: Mike Boyle

Series Editors: Keith Hirst and Lesley Higginbottom

William Collins's dream of knowledge for all began with the publication of his first book in 1819. A self-educated mill worker, he not only enriched millions of lives, but also founded a flourishing publishing house. Today, staying true to this spirit, Collins books are packed with inspiration, innovation and practical expertise. They place you at the centre of a world of possibility and give you exactly what you need to explore it.

Collins. Freedom to teach.

Published by Collins
An imprint of HarperCollinsPublishers
77-85 Fulham Palace Road
Hammersmith
London
W6 8JB

Browse the complete Collins catalogue at
www.collinseducation.com

British Library Cataloguing in Publication Data. A Catalogue record for this publication is available from the British Library.

Commissioned by Penny Fowler
Series Editors Keith Hirst and Lesley Higginbottom
Project Managed by Alexandra Riley
Edited by Rachel Hutchings
Proof read by Camilla Behrens
Design by Newgen Imaging
Cover design by Angela English
Production by Arjen Jansen
Printed and bound in Hong Kong by Printing Express

Mixed Sources
Product group from well-managed
forests and other controlled sources
www.fsc.org Cert no. SW-COC-1806
© 1996 Forest Stewardship Council

FSC is a non-profit international organisation established to promote the responsible management of the world's forests. Products carrying the FSC label are independently certified to assure consumers that they come from forests that are managed to meet the social, economic and ecological needs of present and future generations.

Find out more about HarperCollins and the environment at
www.harpercollins.co.uk/green

Contents

Introduction

Topics at a glance. This may help you plan your revision:

Topic	Revised
Stimulus and response; tropisms, taxes and kineses; reflex arc	
Control of heartbeat	
Receptors, Pacinian corpuscle and retina	
Hormones, local chemical mediators and plant growth substances	
Neurones, action potentials and synapses	
Skeletal muscle	
Homeostasis and negative feedback	
Temperature control	
Blood glucose and diabetes	
Oestrus cycle	
The genetic code and protein synthesis	
Mutation	
Control of gene expression	
DNA technology including gene therapy, stem cells and DNA sequencing; ethical issues	
Medical diagnosis and DNA profiling	

What the examiners are looking for

It is important to know what skills the examiners must test. You can find them in an often-overlooked section of the specification called *Assessment Objectives* (AOs).

To save you looking, they are:

- AO1. 30% of marks. **Knowledge and understanding of science and How Science Works.** Questions covering this objective will ask you to recognise, recall and show understanding.

- AO2. 40% of marks. **Application of knowledge and understanding of science and How Science Works**. Here you will find words such as analyse, evaluate, apply and assess. These are more advanced skills than simply 'learning the stuff' and are not something that you can put off until revision time. You need to practise them throughout the course so that they become second nature.

- AO3. 30% of marks. **How Science Works** – this is largely the practical work.

So, in the A2 course more weighting is given to AO2 than to AO1. This means that it is very important from the start to practise the interpretation and analysis of data, including the use of statistical tests. Many of the questions at the end of the book give an opportunity to practise these skills.

3.5.1 Stimuli, both internal and external, are detected and lead to a response

A feature of all organisms is the ability to detect and respond to changes in their surroundings.

A **stimulus** is a change in an organism's environment (internal or external) that can be detected by receptor cells.

A **receptor** is a specialised cell that detects a stimulus and initiates a nerve impulse. Some receptors exist as individual cells (many are found in the skin, for example) while other receptors are concentrated in sense organs, such as the eye.

Taxes and **kineses** are simple behavioural responses seen in organisms that can move; for example, animals or aquatic organisms that can swim in a particular direction.

A **kinesis** is a change in the speed of random movement in response to environmental stimulus. This is seen in organisms such as woodlice. If placed in bright, dry conditions (Fig 1) they move about at random until they find somewhere that is darker and more humid, when their movements slow down or stop.

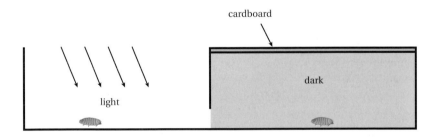

cardboard

dark

light

Fig 1
A simple choice chamber can be used to provide a variety of choices, most commonly light/dark and dry/humid. The woodlice cannot detect the direction of the stimuli, but they move around until, by chance, they find the conditions they prefer

A **taxis** is a directed movement toward or away from a stimulus. There are positive and negative taxes. For example, many types of maggots can detect and move away from light, an example of a negative phototaxis (i.e. phototaxis is when a whole organism moves in response to the stimulus of light). The key difference is that taxes are directional responses, while kineses are non directional.

Tropisms are usually seen in plants, which have no muscles but can respond by growing in a particular direction (page 13). Movement is slow (by human standards) and brought about by control of cell division and elongation. There are several different tropisms. Common tropisms include chemotropism (chemicals), gravitropism/geotropism (gravity), hydrotropism (water), phototropism (lights or colours of light) and thigmotropism (touch). Movement *towards* a stimulus is a positive tropism; *away* is negative.

Essential Notes

Your *dorsal* side is your back,
Your *ventral* side is your front.

Reflex arcs

A **reflex** is a fixed movement of some part of an animal in response to a particular stimulus. Blinking and the knee jerk are familiar examples. The essential components of a reflex are:

- **Sensory neurone** – a nerve cell that carries impulses from a receptor to the central nervous system.

- **Central nervous system** (CNS) – the brain and spinal cord. The CNS processes incoming information and produces a response, often based on previous experience.

- **Motor neurone** – a nerve cell that carries impulses from the CNS to the effectors.

- **Effectors** – organs that bring about a response, usually muscles or glands.

Fig 2
The reflex arc represents the most direct way of connecting a sense organ to an effector, producing the fastest possible response

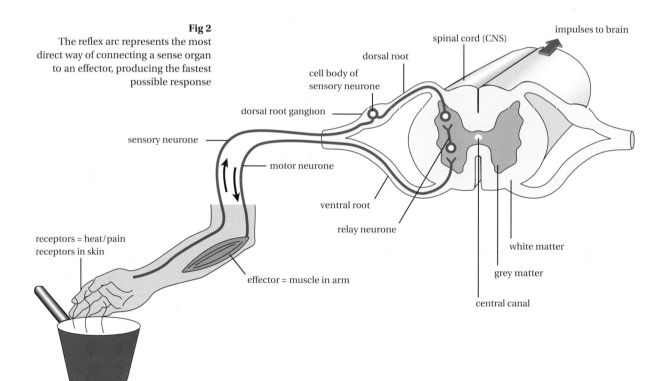

The **reflex arc** is the simplest example of coordination, for example, blinking. A particular stimulus leads to a fixed response – this is very rapid and cannot be controlled because the nerve impulses involved do not pass through the conscious parts of the brain.

Fig 2 shows an example of a reflex that avoids danger (in this case, heat) and minimises damage to the body. Other reflexes, such as the knee jerk, are postural reflexes; one of the many mechanisms we use to maintain our position and body control without having to constantly think about fine adjustments. Most reflexes are either postural or have evolved to avoid danger.

The knee jerk reaction is a three-neurone reflex arc. In this example the reflex is initiated by the stretch receptor in the patellar tendon. A tap in this tendon, just below the knee, causes the lower leg to kick forwards.

The three neurones involved are:

- A **sensory neurone** that links the receptor with the spinal cord.
- A short **relay neurone** that connects the incoming and outgoing neurones.
- The **motor neurone** that transmits impulses to the effector.

Sensory information that the knee jerk has happened also passes up the spinal cord to the brain. The response happens well before the conscious brain has a chance to stop it, but one is aware that the leg has moved.

NB: Some studies have shown that only two neurones are involved, so the sensory neurone connects directly to the motor neurone. Others show that at least one relay neurone is involved. (Do not worry too much about this.)

The control of heartbeat

The heart is **myogenic**, meaning that the muscle contraction originates from within the heart muscle itself. When the nerves leading to the heart are severed, it continues to beat at a slow, regular pace, but cannot be matched to the changing needs of the body. The **cardiovascular centre** in the medulla of the brain is responsible for matching heart rate to the needs of the body, but it modifies rather than initiates the beat.

The cardiovascular centre receives information from two main sources:

- The *carotid* and *aortic bodies* contain *chemoreceptor* cells that are sensitive to carbon dioxide levels in the plasma. When carbon dioxide levels rise, for example, during exercise, impulses pass more frequently to the cardiovascular centre.
- Pressure receptors (*baroreceptors*) in the *carotid sinus* transmit impulses to the cardiovascular centre when blood pressure rises. This is an essential part of the **negative feedback** system that keeps blood pressure within certain limits, thus avoiding low or high blood pressure.

There are two *antagonistic* nerves (Fig 3) leading from the cardiovascular centre to the **sino-atrial node**:

- a *sympathetic nerve*, carrying impulses that speed up the heart.
- a *parasympathetic nerve*, carrying impulses that slow down the heart.

The **sympathetic nervous system (SNS)** and the **parasympathetic nervous system (PSNS)** form part of the autonomic nervous system (ANS).

When we exercise, increased carbon dioxide levels are detected and impulses are transmitted to the medulla. In response, impulses pass down the sympathetic nerve to the heart to increase the rate of the heartbeat.

Essential Notes

The term antagonistic means 'opposing effects' and can apply to nerves, muscles or hormones.

Examiners' Notes

Remember that the brain only *modifies* the rate of heartbeat.

Fig 3
Two nerves pass from the cardiovascular centre to the heart. If these nerves are cut, the heart continues to beat, but its rate cannot be modified

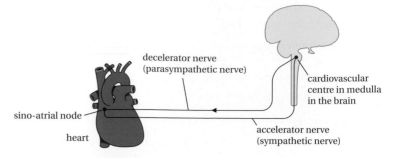

The Pacinian corpuscle, an example of a receptor

The **Pacinian corpuscle** is a receptor found deep in mammalian skin, where its function is to detect pressure and vibration – it is a *mechanoreceptor*. Each corpuscle consists of a single sensory neurone (often described as a 'nerve ending') surrounded by 20–60 lamellae (layers) of fibrous connective tissue separated by viscous gel (Fig 4).

A change in pressure on the corpuscle is transmitted through to the sensory nerve, which deforms, causing *stretch-mediated sodium ion channels* in the axon membrane to open. This allows sodium ions to diffuse in, creating a *generator potential*. If this potential reaches a certain level, known as a *threshold*, an impulse will pass down the sensory nerve. If the stimulus is too small, only a small amount of sodium will diffuse in, the threshold is not reached and no impulse is generated. The greater the stimulus, the higher the frequency of the impulses.

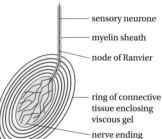

Fig 4
A cross-section through a Pacinian corpuscle. The layers of gel act as shock absorbers, preventing the receptor from being stimulated for more than a brief moment

From this it can be seen that Pacinian corpuscles will detect *changes* of pressure, but not prolonged pressure. The gel acts as a 'shock absorber' and quickly allows the sensory nerve to assume its normal shape. This is called *adaptation*. No more impulses will be generated until the pressure changes again. This is an important point about receptors – they will generally respond to changes in environment, not constant stimuli.

The retina

The **retina** is a single layer of light-sensitive receptor cells – *rods* and *cones* – together with connecting neurones on the back of the eye (Figs 5a and 5b). The overall function of the retina is to gather information about the incoming light and relay it to the brain via the *optic nerve*. The actual image is formed in the brain, in the *visual cortex*.

Fig 5a
The structures of the eye and their functions

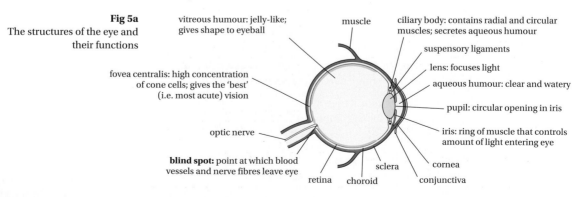

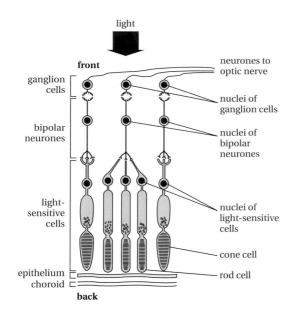

Fig 5b
The arrangement of receptor cells in the retina

Rods and cones differ in both their sensitivity and **visual acuity** (Table 1). Sensitivity refers to the level of light needed for the cells to function, while acuity refers to their ability to perceive detail. Rods are more sensitive than cones and can function even in dim light. There are two reasons for this greater sensitivity:

1   The pigment in rod cells is more easily bleached (broken down) than the pigment in the cones.

2   **Retinal convergence** – many rod cells converge into one neurone (Fig 6), so they can all contribute to the generator potential, making it more likely that the threshold will be reached; this is called *summation*.

Feature	Rod cells	Cone cells
Shape	Rod-shaped outer segment	Cone-shaped outer segment
Connections	Many rods converge into one neurone	Only a single cone per neurone at centre of fovea
Visual acuity	Low	High
Visual pigments	**Rhodopsin**	**Iodopsin**
Numbers	120 million per retina	Seven million per retina
Distribution	Found evenly all over retina	All over retina, but more concentrated towards fovea; the fovea itself consists only of cones
Sensitivity	Sensitive to low light intensity	Only functions in bright light
Overall function	Black-and-white vision in poor light	Seeing colour and detail in bright light

Table 1
The differences between rods and cones

Fig 6
The concept of retinal convergence. The cones would send impulses to the brain that would be perceived as two separate images, while the rods would show just one image

two separate impulses to brain

one impulse to brain

two separate images fall on cones in fovea

two separate images fall on rods in periphery of retina

Visual acuity

Visual acuity is the ability to distinguish objects that are close together. For instance, these lines 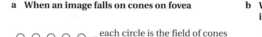 appear as two separate lines, but if you look at them from a distance they appear to blend into one thicker line. The greater the distance at which we can distinguish two lines the greater our visual acuity.

Although both rods and cones enable us to see, it is the cones that give us our high visual acuity. For example, if the letter E were to fall on the cones, we would clearly distinguish it as a letter E; if it were to fall on the rods, we would just see a blob (Fig 7).

Fig 7
Visual acuity and the fovea

a When an image falls on cones on fovea

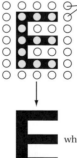

each circle is the field of cones which converge into one neurone in the optic nerve (at the centre of fovea, 1 cone = 1 neurone); the neurones coloured yellow are those which 'fire' as a result of the image

what the brain 'perceives'

b When the same image falls on rods in periphery of retina

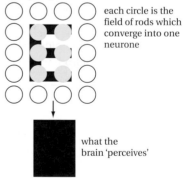

each circle is the field of rods which converge into one neurone

what the brain 'perceives'

The main reason for the difference in visual acuity between the rods and cones is retinal convergence. Fig 6 shows that several rods all converge on one neurone, but each cone has its own connection. Any impulses generated by an individual cone are transmitted to the brain but any impulses generated by a rod are fed into a neurone along with impulses from many others.

The greatest concentration of cones is at a point on the retina called the **fovea**. It is only when light falls on this point that we can see things in detail (Fig 7a).

The key idea about visual acuity is that cones send more information to the brain *per unit area* of retina than is sent by the rod cells.

3.5.2 Coordination may be chemical or electrical in nature

Animals, which by definition are multicellular, need some method of internal communication. This can be achieved either by nerves or by **hormones**.

Hormones

Hormones:

- are chemicals
- are made by endocrine glands (which have no duct/delivery tube, and secrete directly into the bloodstream)
- travel in the blood
- have an effect on particular *target cells* or *target organs*.

Many hormones are *peptides*, that is, chains of amino acids, and some are lipids, in which case they are known as *steroids*. The peptide hormones are water soluble while the steroids are lipid soluble. This is an important distinction because they work in fundamentally different ways.

Mode of action of hormones

Most hormones are water soluble and travel in solution in the blood. When they encounter a cell with the correct receptor protein they fit into the receptor, *but they do not enter the cell*. Instead, the binding activates an enzyme inside the cell, **adenyl cyclase**, which in turn converts ATP in the cytoplasm into **cyclic AMP** (adenosine monophosphate) which acts as a *second messenger*, the hormone itself being the first messenger. Cyclic AMP brings about an effect by activating specific enzymes or enzyme pathways. Both **insulin** and **glucagon** act in this way – see 'Regulation of blood glucose levels' on page 27.

Lipid hormones are known as steroids and are based on the cholesterol molecule. Familiar steroids include **oestrogen**, **progesterone** and testosterone. These are different from water-soluble hormones because, being lipids,

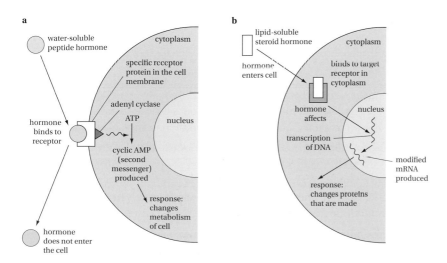

a

water-soluble peptide hormone

cytoplasm

specific receptor protein in the cell membrane

adenyl cyclase

ATP

nucleus

hormone binds to receptor

cyclic AMP (second messenger) produced

response: changes metabolism of cell

hormone does not enter the cell

b

lipid-soluble steroid hormone

cytoplasm

hormone enters cell

binds to target receptor in cytoplasm

hormone affects

nucleus

transcription of DNA

modified mRNA produced

response: changes proteins that are made

Fig 8
Mode of action of hormones
a Water-soluble hormones work via a second messenger which is formed inside the cell when the hormone binds to its membrane receptor
b Steroid hormones bind to a receptor in the cytoplasm; the hormone/ receptor complex enters the nucleus and binds directly to the DNA, altering gene expression; genes can be activated or de-activated, thereby changing the proteins made by the cell

they can pass straight through the cell membrane. There is no need for a second messenger – once inside the cell they combine with a target receptor molecule in the cytoplasm. This hormone/receptor complex passes into the nucleus where it directly affects gene expression (Fig 8). The mode of action of oestrogen is covered in more detail on page 46.

In contrast, nervous communication is brought about by electrical signals called *impulses*, which are transmitted down elongated specialised cells called **neurones**. The essential differences between nerves and hormones are shown in Table 2.

Table 2
The main differences between nervous and hormonal communication

Property	Nervous system	Hormonal system
Nature of signal	Impulses are ionic/ electrical charge; chemical transmission at synapses	Chemical
Size of signal	Frequency modulated – determined by number of impulses sent along an axon, and the number of axons stimulated	Amplitude modulated – determined by concentration of hormone
Speed of signal	Very rapid – usually a fraction of a second	Usually slower; insulin takes minutes to act; **adrenaline** is very fast acting (with good reason)
Duration of signal	Very short lived	Often prolonged
Precision of signal	Very precise – for example, one part of one muscle	Often general; hormones can affect many different areas of the body at the same time
Capacity for modification	Can be modified by previous experience ('learning')	Cannot be modified by previous experience

Essential Notes

Most hormones are broken down by the liver so they do not carry on having an effect long after they have been secreted. If hormones did have a long-term effect once secretion had stopped, it would make hormonal control much less precise. Prolonged hormone action can only be achieved by prolonged secretion. A good example of this is the human growth hormone, *somatotropin*, which exerts its effect for years during childhood.

Local chemical mediators

There are many other substances made by cells that have a particular effect on surrounding cells without travelling in the blood. These are known as *local chemical mediators* rather than hormones. Common examples include:

- **Histamine** – this is released by a particular type of white cell known as a mast cell, and by many other cells in response to damage. Histamine causes the familiar symptoms of allergy such as inflammation, mucus secretion, swelling and itching. Hence, the use of antihistamines to treat the symptoms of allergy.

- **Prostaglandins** – so named because they were first discovered in secretions from the prostate gland (that is, in semen), this group of lipid compounds have a variety of functions including contraction and relaxation of smooth muscle, the dilation and constriction of blood vessels, control of blood pressure and degree of inflammation.

Plant hormones

There are several classes of substances that act as plant growth regulators, controlling various activities such as germination, patterns of growth, flowering, fruiting and ripening. They are often known as hormones because they are made on one part of a plant and have an effect on a different part.

Auxins such as *indole acetic acid* (*IAA*) are important substances that control many different aspects of plant growth including tropisms, differentiation of tissues and abscission (leaf and fruit fall). The experiments that clarified the role of IAA in phototropism are outlined in Figs 9a and 9b.

The first well-documented investigations into phototropism were performed by Charles Darwin and his son Francis in the 1880s. They had observed plants bending towards light and wanted to find out which part of the plant was light-sensitive. The Darwins' experiment is shown in Fig 9a. Father and son worked with grass seedlings, which have a protective covering over the young stem called a *coleoptile*. The two men illuminated the seedlings from one side, and 'blindfolded' different parts of the coleoptile.

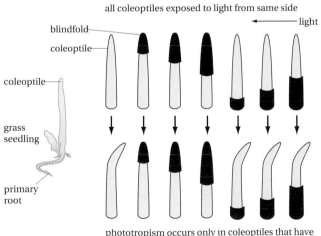

Fig 9a
The Darwins' experiment

The conclusion the Darwins' reached was that there must be a message, produced in the tip, which passes down the stem and causes the bending. Plants do not have neurones and so any communication must be chemical in nature.

The Dutch biologist Frits Warmolt Went succeeded in isolating the substance responsible. One of his early experiments is shown in Fig 9b. This substance was given the name auxin (from the Greek *auxein* – to increase; or *auxano* – to grow) and when the chemical nature of this substance was investigated it was found to be *indole acetic acid* (*IAA*).

Fig 9b
Went's experiment
A coleoptile is illuminated and the auxin collected in a gelatin block; when the block is placed on a non-illuminated coleoptile the same curvature is seen

1 Tip removed and placed on gelatin

2 Gelatin placed on one edge of another decapitated coleoptile

3 Substance diffuses down one side from gelatin

4 Coleoptile curves away from gelatin as it grows

diffusion of growth substance

gelatin

oat coleoptile

It was assumed that auxin diffuses down the stem from its site of production. When illuminated from one side, auxin accumulates on the dark side and diffuses downwards, promoting the cell elongation that bends the coleoptiles towards the light.

Auxin has a key role to play in growth following germination. Seeds are scattered in the ground and may germinate at any angle. However, the root must grow down and the shoot must grow upwards. Studies have shown that auxin is responsible for controlling this *geotropism* (Fig 10).

Fig 10
Geotropism
The seedling is responding to gravity: the shoot is negatively geotropic and the root is positively geotropic; these movements are controlled by auxin, which accumulates on the underside of the seedling

root hairs

if a plant is laid on its side, auxin gathers in lower half of stem and root

auxin slows growth in root, so root curves downwards

auxin stimulates growth in shoot, so stem curves upwards

The graph shows that at the concentrations found in the seedlings, auxin inhibits root growth and stimulates shoot growth. In the shoot, cell division and elongation along the underside are stimulated, so growth is upwards; in the root, the opposite is true

Essential Notes

This is a logarithmic scale, which simply allows a large range of concentrations to fit onto one graph.

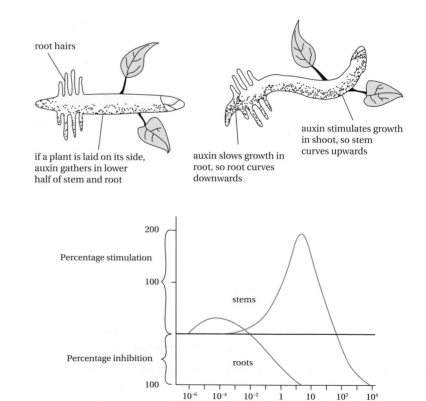

Percentage stimulation

200

100

stems

Percentage inhibition

roots

100

10^{-6} 10^{-4} 10^{-2} 1   10 10^{2} 10^{4}

Concentration of auxin (ppm)

Nerve impulses

A **neurone** is a nerve cell, a specialised elongated cell that is capable of carrying impulses from one end to the other. There are several types of neurones but all have the same basic features:

- a **cell body** that contains the nucleus and other organelles
- **dendrites** that take impulses towards the cell body
- an **axon** that takes impulses away from the cell body
- **synapses** that junction with other neurones or effectors (for example, muscles).

Fig 11 shows the basic structure of a motor neurone. Fig 12 shows how the neurone is involved in transmitting impulses. There are two processes to understand: the **resting potential**, which is basically a state of readiness, and the **action potential**, which is another name for the nerve impulse.

Examiners' Notes

Make sure that you can distinguish between a *neurone* (a single nerve cell) and a *nerve* (a bundle of axons surrounded by connective tissue).

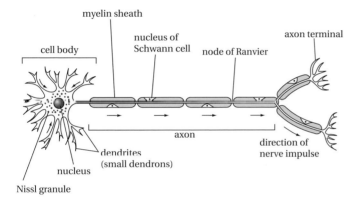

Fig 11
Basic structure of a motor neurone. All neurones have the same basic features, but the positioning of the cell body, and the number and length of the axons and dendrites, vary

The resting potential

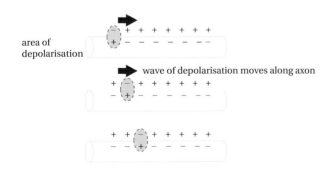

Fig 12
A nerve impulse, or action potential, is a wave of depolarisation that spreads along the axon; the active transport/diffusion combination quickly re-establishes the resting potential once the impulse has passed

The resting potential results from an unequal distribution of ions, brought about by two processes: active transport and facilitated diffusion (see Fig 13a).

1 **Active transport** – all animal cell membranes contain a protein pump called Na^+K^+ATPase. This uses the energy from splitting ATP to pump ions; three sodium ions pass out of the cell and two potassium ions move in. It is an unequal exchange; more positive ions pass out than pass in.

Fig 13a

How a resting potential is set up across an axon membrane

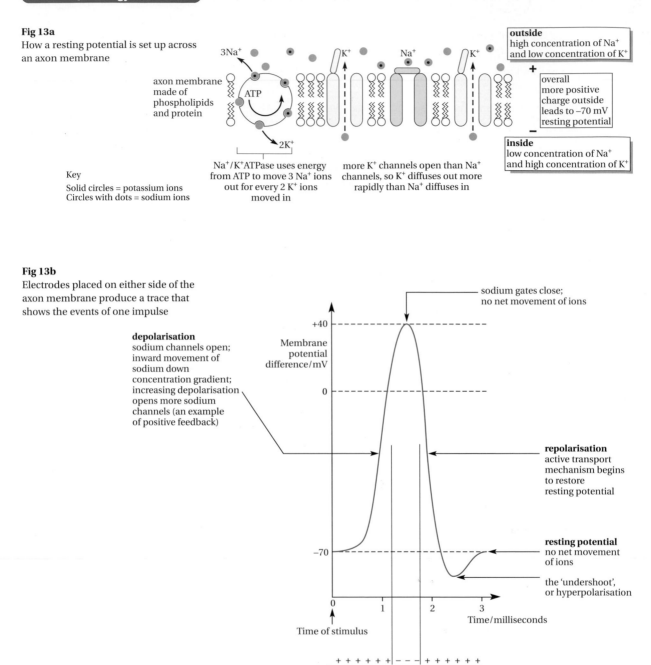

axon membrane made of phospholipids and protein

Key

Solid circles = potassium ions
Circles with dots = sodium ions

Na⁺/K⁺ATPase uses energy from ATP to move 3 Na⁺ ions out for every 2 K⁺ ions moved in

more K⁺ channels open than Na⁺ channels, so K⁺ diffuses out more rapidly than Na⁺ diffuses in

outside
high concentration of Na⁺ and low concentration of K⁺

overall more positive charge outside leads to –70 mV resting potential

inside
low concentration of Na⁺ and high concentration of K⁺

Fig 13b

Electrodes placed on either side of the axon membrane produce a trace that shows the events of one impulse

depolarisation
sodium channels open; inward movement of sodium down concentration gradient; increasing depolarisation opens more sodium channels (an example of positive feedback)

sodium gates close; no net movement of ions

Membrane potential difference/mV

repolarisation
active transport mechanism begins to restore resting potential

resting potential
no net movement of ions

the 'undershoot', or hyperpolarisation

Time of stimulus

Time/milliseconds

action potential
direction of nerve impulse

2 **Faciliated diffusion** – there are also sodium and potassium ion channels (specific proteins) in the membrane. These channels are normally closed, but they 'leak', allowing sodium ions to diffuse in and potassium ions to leak out, down their respective concentration gradients. Generally, the potassium channels are *more leaky* than the sodium channels, so more potassium diffuses out to join the sodium ions that have been actively pumped out.

Together, these two processes cause an imbalance of Na^+ and K^+ ions across the membrane: there are more positive ions outside the axon. This imbalance causes a potential difference across all animal cell membranes, called the **resting potential** or the *membrane potential*. The value of this potential varies from –20 to –200 mV in different cells and species, but is usually about –70 mV.

The action potential

The action potential is generated when the nerve is stimulated. The stimulus might come from a receptor cell (for example, in a sense organ) or another neurone.

The action potential is brought about by a quick reversal in the permeability of the axon membrane, allowing sodium ions to flow into the axon, making the inside positive with respect to the outside (Figs 13a and 13b). The sodium and potassium channels are *voltage gated*, which means that they can change their shape, to let more or fewer ions pass, according to the voltage across the membrane.

The action potential has two stages: depolarisation and repolarisation.

- **Depolarisation** – step by step:

  1 When a neurone is stimulated, the voltage across the axon membrane changes.

  2 A few voltage-gated sodium channels detect this change, opening to allow some sodium to diffuse in.

  3 If the stimulus is large enough to reach the *threshold value* of about –50 mV, the rest of the voltage-gated sodium channels open for about 0.5 ms (half a millisecond, or one two-thousandths of a second).

  4 This causes sodium ions to rapidly diffuse in, making the inside of the cell more positive. This is an example of a **positive feedback** ('change creating more change') – the more Na^+ ions there are, the more the voltage changes, so the more ion channels open, and the more sodium ions diffuse in.

- **Repolarisation** – when the membrane potential reaches 0 V, the potassium channels open for 0.5 ms, causing potassium ions to rush out, making the inside more negative again. Since this restores the original polarity, it is called repolarisation.

Re-establishing the resting potential
The potassium channels remain open until after the resting potential value of –70 mV has been reached. This causes hyperpolarisation (the 'undershoot' on Fig 13b) when the potential difference reaches about –80 mV. The potassium channels then close and the resting potential is established once again.

Essential Notes

Normally there is a balance of positive and negative ions (notably chloride, Cl^-). In neurones, movement of positive ions causes the resting potential.

Refractory period

This is the 'recovery period' after the transmission of an action potential. There are two phases:

- **Absolute refractory period** – this is the time during which it is impossible to create another impulse, no matter how intense the stimulus.

- **Relative refractory period** – this is the time during which it is possible to create another impulse, but the stimulus needs to be greater than normal.

The refractory period is important because it keeps action potentials separate, or discrete, rather than blending together.

Action potential facts:

- An action potential is not an electrical current, nor is it a 'message'.

- All action potentials are the same size; there are no large or small impulses.

- They travel along axons at speeds up to 120 metres per second.

- The speed of transmission depends on the axon diameter (larger = faster), the number of synapses in the pathway (more = slower), temperature (higher = faster, because diffusion is faster) and whether the nerve is myelinated or not.

Saltatory conduction

Saltatory conduction occurs in myelinated nerves, when the action potential 'jumps' from node to node. This greatly increases the speed of transmission. The myelin sheath insulates the axon, and so ion exchange can only occur at the nodes of Ranvier in between the Schwann cells, where the axon membrane is exposed.

When the action potential is present at one node, the influx of Na^+ ions causes the displacement of K^+ ions down the axon (like charges repel). This diffusion of K^+ down the axon makes the next node more positive and depolarises it until the threshold is reached. In this way the impulse quickly jumps from node to node at speeds of over 100 metres per second, 10 times faster than the best sprinters. Saltatory conduction, from the Latin *saltare* meaning to jump, means jumping conduction.

As well as being faster than non-myelinated conduction, saltatory conduction is very energy efficient in terms of ATP usage. Only a small part of the axon is involved in the exchange of ions, so far fewer ions need to be pumped back after the action potential has passed.

The synapse

Synapses are gaps between neurones. They are a vital component of the nervous system because they allow the selection of different pathways for the transmission of impulses. All our thoughts, memories, skills and actions are only possible because synapses allow us to select complex neural pathways.

The events of synaptic transmission are described as follows and in Fig 14:

1 The action potential arrives at the *synaptic knob*.

2 Calcium channels open, so Ca^{2+} ions flow into the synaptic knob.

3 The calcium ions cause vesicles containing a **transmitter substance** to move to the *presynaptic membrane*.

Examiners' Notes

Always refer to action potentials as *impulses*, not messages. Messages are complex, whereas nerve impulses are simply electrical 'blips'.

Impulses do not cross synapses. An impulse comes to an end once it reaches a synapse. After synaptic transmission, a new impulse is generated.

Essential Notes

Calcium ions are actively pumped out of the synaptic knob between impulses so that there is a diffusion gradient. When an impulse arrives, calcium channels open so calcium diffuses in; after that, it is pumped out again.

4 The vesicles fuse with the presynaptic membrane and discharge the transmitter into the *synaptic cleft*.

5 Molecules of transmitter diffuse across the gap and fit into specific receptor sites on the *postsynaptic membrane*.

6 The permeability of the postsynaptic membrane changes, causing a movement of ions. Na$^+$ ions flow inwards, building up a charge known as **EPSP** (excitatory postsynaptic potential).

7 If the EPSP reaches a threshold, an action potential is generated in the neurone.

8 The transmitter substance is broken down by an enzyme in the cleft.

9 The products of breakdown are reabsorbed into the synaptic knob, where they are re-synthesised using energy from ATP synthesised by the mitochondria.

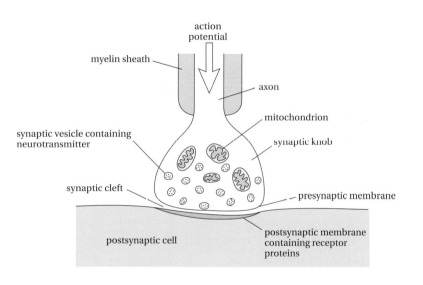

Fig 14a
The basic structure of the synapse

Fig 14b
The sequence of events (1–9) in chemical transmission at a synapse

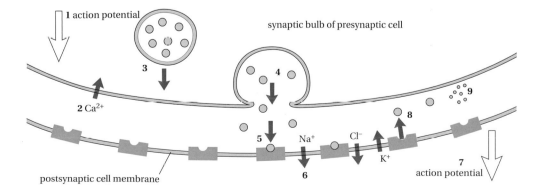

Examiners' Notes

Many drugs and toxins work by affecting synaptic transmission in some way. You are not expected to learn the mode of action of a wide variety of drugs and toxins. Exam questions will test your understanding of synaptic transmission (outlined on the previous pages) by using the example of a particular drug or toxin.

NB: All the events in synaptic transmission take place in about one hundredth of a second. Transmission across synapses is *unidirectional* (in one direction only), because the transmitter is made only on the presynaptic side and the receptor proteins are found only on the postsynaptic side. This prevents impulses being transmitted in the wrong direction.

The most widespread transmitter is **acetylcholine (Ach)**, which is found in the synapses of most voluntary nerves, including nerve–muscle junctions. The sympathetic nervous system (SNS) uses **noradrenaline**, while the brain has many different transmitters, including *serotonin* and *dopamine*.

Synapses that release acetylcholine are said to be **cholinergic synapses**. In these synapses the enzyme **acetylcholinesterase** is found in the cleft, where it breaks down the transmitter once the impulse has been generated. This prevents prolonged stimulation. Acetylcholine is broken down into choline and acetic acid, which are re-absorbed into the presynaptic membrane where they are re-combined into active transmitter. A synapse that releases noradrenaline is said to be an **adrenergic synapse**.

Inhibition at synapses

If every nerve impulse that arrived at a synapse succeeded in setting up impulses in the next neurone, the result would be chaos. The significance of synapses is that they allow us to select particular pathways. Thus, at any one time many more synapses need inhibiting than need stimulating. For this reason there are inhibitory neurones. Impulses arriving at synapses of inhibitory neurones make it more difficult for an action potential to be generated. The neurotransmitters from these synapses open potassium and chloride channels rather than sodium channels, and the resulting ion movement causes an **IPSP** (inhibitory postsynaptic potential) in which the postsynaptic membranes are hyperpolarised (to about –90 mV) rather than depolarised. The balance of inhibition and stimulation received at a particular synapse will determine whether an action potential is generated or not.

Temporal and spatial summation

Summation means 'to add up' and refers to the fact that any particular action potential arriving at a synapse might not be enough to generate an action potential in the postsynaptic neurone, but two or more might. There are two types of summation:

- **Temporal summation** ('in time') – where two or more impulses arrive in quick succession *down the same neurone.*
- **Spatial summation** ('in space') – where two or more impulses arrive at the *same time down different neurones.*

In both cases, summation is achieved because each impulse causes more transmitter to be released, contributing to the EPSP and making it more likely that the threshold will be reached.

3.5.3 Skeletal muscles are stimulated to contract by nerves and act as effectors

Muscle is a remarkable tissue that has the ability to contract. Broadly speaking there are three types of muscle in the body: smooth, cardiac and skeletal, as follows:

1 **Smooth muscle** – is generally found in tubular organs such as the intestines, blood vessels and reproductive system where its function is peristalsis.

2 **Cardiac muscle** – is only found in the heart.

3 **Skeletal muscle** – is attached to bones where its function is to produce movement and maintain posture. Contraction of skeletal muscle is the key topic you need to learn.

Skeletal muscle

Fig 15 overleaf shows the basic structure of skeletal muscle. The key unit is the **sarcomere** – one short length of a muscle fibre in which the pattern of bands is repeated. The changes in this banding pattern when muscle contracts reveal a lot about muscular contraction, making it a favourite topic for exam questions.

Some skeletal muscle facts:

- An individual muscle is made up of hundreds of cylindrical *muscle fibres*, about 50 μm in diameter and ranging in length from a few millimetres to several centimetres.

- Muscle fibres are not composed of individual cells – the cell membranes have broken down and so each fibre has many nuclei.

- Each fibre is surrounded by a modified cell membrane called the *sarcolemma*.

- Each muscle fibre is composed of many long, cylindrical *myofibrils*, consisting of a repeating arrangement of proteins, which causes the banding pattern.

- Each repeated pattern of proteins is called a sarcomere.

- The two main proteins involved in muscular contraction are **actin** (thin) and **myosin** (thick) filaments.

- Muscles contract when the actin fibres are pulled over the myosin fibres.

- Two other proteins involved are **tropomyosin**, and **troponin**.

Tropomyosin winds around the actin filament, preventing it from binding to myosin. Troponin, a globular protein, moves the tropomyosin out of the way. This allows actin to bind to myosin, thus initiating muscular contraction.

Within each sarcomere there are two light bands: the I zone consisting of only actin filaments, and the H zone that consists of only myosin. Between them are darker areas where these proteins overlap. When muscles contract, the actin and myosin filaments are pulled over each other so that the light bands get smaller. Note that the width of the dark band corresponds to the width of the myosin molecules, so it does not get any narrower – molecules do not shrink, they just slide over each other.

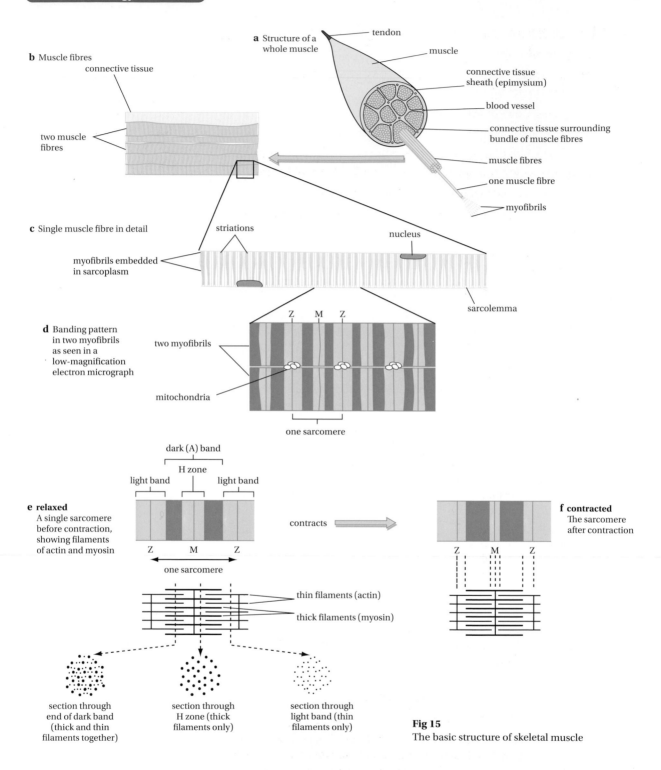

a Structure of a whole muscle

tendon

muscle

connective tissue sheath (epimysium)

blood vessel

connective tissue surrounding bundle of muscle fibres

muscle fibres

one muscle fibre

myofibrils

b Muscle fibres

connective tissue

two muscle fibres

c Single muscle fibre in detail

striations

nucleus

myofibrils embedded in sarcoplasm

sarcolemma

d Banding pattern in two myofibrils as seen in a low-magnification electron micrograph

Z M Z

two myofibrils

mitochondria

one sarcomere

dark (A) band

H zone

light band   light band

e relaxed
A single sarcomere before contraction, showing filaments of actin and myosin

contracts

Z   M   Z

one sarcomere

f contracted
The sarcomere after contraction

Z   M   Z

thin filaments (actin)

thick filaments (myosin)

section through end of dark band (thick and thin filaments together)

section through H zone (thick filaments only)

section through light band (thin filaments only)

Fig 15
The basic structure of skeletal muscle

The sliding filament theory of muscle contraction

The basic steps in muscular contraction:

1   An impulse arrives down a motor nerve and terminates at the **neuromuscular junction** (a modified synapse).

2   The synapse secretes acetylcholine.

3   Acetylcholine fits into receptor sites on the *motor end plate*.

4   The binding causes a change in the permeability of the **sarcoplasmic reticulum**, resulting in an influx of calcium ions into the *myofilament*.

5   The calcium ions bind to the troponin, changing its shape.

6   Troponin displaces the tropomyosin, so that the myosin heads can bind to the actin.

7   The myosin head pulls backwards, so that the actin is pulled over the myosin. This is the 'power stroke'.

8   An ATP molecule becomes fixed to the myosin head, causing it to detach from the actin.

9   The splitting of ATP provides the energy to move the myosin head back to its original position, 'cocking the trigger' again.

10   The myosin head again becomes attached to the actin, but further along.

11   In this way, the actin is quickly pulled over the myosin in a ratchet motion, shortening the sarcomere, the whole filament and the muscle.

The role of ATP and phosphocreatine

The energy for muscular contraction comes from ATP, but during intense exercise the ATP runs out after about three seconds. After this, ATP is quickly re-synthesised using phosphate derived from the splitting of *phosphocreatine* (*PC*). The ATP/PC system can provide enough energy for maximum effort – a sprint, for example – for up to 10 seconds. After this, for up to about one minute, ATP is supplied from glycolysis, the first stage of respiration. This second system can still provide enough energy for maximum effort, but it is anaerobic, and lactate build up is a painful problem.

After about a minute, supplies of ATP come from full aerobic respiration. The disadvantage of aerobic respiration is that it can only provide ATP quickly enough for exercise at about 60%–70% of maximum capacity, but the good news is that this system can keep going as long as there is fuel (glucose or lipid) and there is no build up of lactate.

Slow- and fast-twitch muscle fibres

There are two different types of skeletal muscle fibres:

* **Fast-twitch fibres** contract quickly and powerfully, but fatigue quickly. They rely on glycolysis for their ATP, and so lactate builds up rapidly. Athletes who specialise in power events such as short sprints, throwing, jumping and weightlifting tend to have more fast-twitch fibres.

Essential Notes

Sarcoplasmic reticulum is modified endoplasmic reticulum a network of membranes had surround the myofilaments.

Essential Notes

Phosphocreatine is also called creatine phosphate, so in this context PC and CP can refer to the same substance.

- **Slow-twitch fibres** contract more slowly, producing less power, but they have the advantage of not tiring so quickly and so they can keep going for long periods. Slow-twitch fibres rely on aerobic respiration for their ATP, and have more mitochondria than fast-twitch fibres.

Individuals are born with a certain balance of fast- and slow-twitch fibres. It is thought that training can alter the balance but there is no conclusive proof of this.

3.5.4 Homeostasis is the maintenance of a constant internal environment

Homeostasis is the ability of an organism to maintain its internal conditions within certain limits. In humans, examples of homeostasis include:

- maintaining the pH of blood and body fluids between 7.3 and 7.45
- maintaining the core body temperature at around 37 °C
- maintaining blood glucose levels between 4 and 11 millimoles per litre.

You can see from these examples that internal conditions are not absolutely constant, but are maintained within fairly narrow limits.

There are many other examples of homeostasis, such as the maintenance of all the different hormone levels and the many components of blood plasma. You need to know about the control of core temperature, blood glucose levels and the female menstrual cycle.

Examiners' Notes

When you discuss an example of homeostasis – in longer exam questions, for example – it is important to consider all of the following:

1 What causes the level to change?

2 What detects the change?

3 How is the change reversed?

Negative feedback – the mechanism of homeostasis

Most examples of homeostasis involve negative feedback. When a factor changes, the homeostatic mechanism acts to reverse that change and bring things back to normal. Fig 16 shows a negative feedback loop and how it differs from positive feedback.

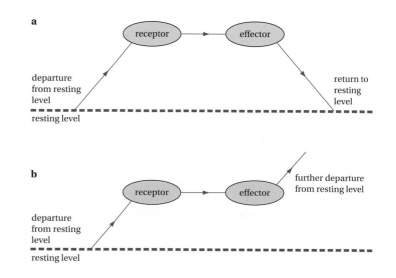

Fig 16
A negative feedback loop and how it differs from positive feedback

a Negative feedback is a mechanism that keeps levels constant
b In contrast, positive feedback is a mechanism for bringing about change

Regulation of body temperature

Regulating body temperature involves the internal generation of heat (as a by-product of metabolic reactions) and the control of its release into the environment. When we are too hot, we maximise our heat loss to the environment, and when we are too cold, we minimise it. We can also alter our metabolic rate to produce more or less heat in the first place.

Some terms:

- **Endotherm** means 'heat from within'. Mammals and birds are endotherms. They can usually control their core temperature regardless of the external temperature. Endotherms control their body temperature by physiological and behavioural means. Endotherms used to be described by the now outdated term 'warm-blooded'.

- **Ectotherm** means 'heat from the outside' and refers to animals, such as amphibians and reptiles, that can only regulate their body temperature by behavioural means. In practice their body temperature is usually similar to that of their environment. Ectotherms used to be described by the now outdated term 'cold-blooded'.

Behavioural thermoregulation in mammals

Although mammals and birds have physiological ways of controlling their core temperature, their behaviour still plays a large part. When humans feel cold, for example, we change our posture and surroundings by possibly folding our arms, putting on more clothes or by closing a window.

The temperature of the blood is detected by the **hypothalamus**, which can be thought of as the body's thermostat. Inside the hypothalamus is the *thermoregulatory centre*, which has two parts; a *heat loss* centre and a *heat gain* centre. Fig 17 gives an overview of the mechanisms of thermoregulation.

The skin plays an important role in thermoregulation, and its structure is shown in Fig 18 overleaf.

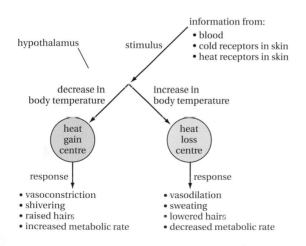

Fig 17
The role of the heat gain centre and heat loss centre of the hypothalamus in temperature regulation

Fig 18
The structure of human skin

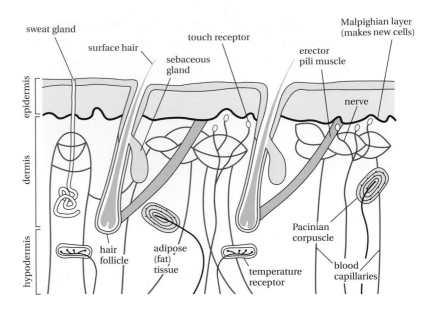

We get too cold when the heat loss from our bodies exceeds what is generated and the temperature of the blood falls. This drop is detected by the hypothalamus, and signals pass from the heat gain centre to bring about the following responses:

1 **Shivering** – rapid contraction and relaxation of the muscles creates heat, which is distributed to the rest of the body in the blood.

2 **Vasoconstriction** – constriction of the muscular arteriole walls re-directs blood away from the skin, keeping the warmer blood in the centre of the body (see a of Fig 19).

3 **Making your hair stand on end** – hairs are raised by means of erector pili muscles. In hairy mammals this traps a layer of insulating air, but in humans it just gives us 'goose pimples'.

Fig 19
Blood flow to the skin can be altered by controlling the flow of blood in the arterioles leading to the surface capillaries

4 **Increasing basal metabolic rate (BMR)** – in the short term, this is achieved by the hormone adrenaline and, in the long term, by secretion of the hormone thyroxine.

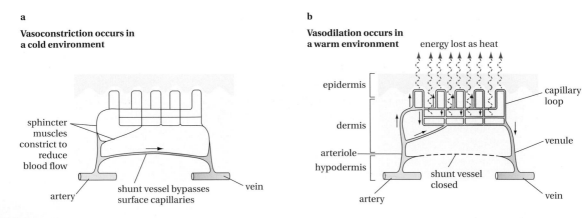

a

Vasoconstriction occurs in a cold environment

b

Vasodilation occurs in a warm environment

We get too hot when we generate more heat than we lose. During exercise, for example, the temperature of the blood rises. In this case, the heat loss centre brings about the following responses:

1 **Sweating** – secretion of a salty solution from the millions of sweat (*sudorific*) glands that cover our bodies. Sweat cools the body as it evaporates (water has a high latent heat of evaporation, which means that water molecules take a lot of energy with them as they change state from liquid to vapour).

2 **Vasodilation** – the arterioles dilate, allowing more blood to flow through the capillaries of the skin. The heat in the blood is transferred to the sweat, and is lost from the body as the sweat evaporates (see b of Fig 19).

3 **Lowering of hairs** – this happens as the erector pili muscles relax.

4 **Basal metabolic rate** – this decreases.

We tend to overheat when we exercise because movement of muscles creates heat. It is basic thermodynamics: no energy conversion is ever 100% efficient – some energy is always lost as heat. Exercise involves two energy conversions: first, when chemical energy in glucose is transferred to ATP via respiration and, second, when the energy in the ATP is used to produce movement in muscles.

Regulation of blood glucose levels

Blood glucose levels need to be kept within certain limits. Glucose is the body's main respiratory fuel, so while a plentiful supply should be in circulation, too much glucose lowers the water potential of the blood.

Too much blood glucose – *hyperglycaemia* – will lower the water potential of the blood and produce symptoms of thirst and (as a result of fluid intake) frequent urination. In contrast, too little glucose, *hypoglycaemia* – will produce symptoms of dizziness, tiredness, lack of concentration, irritability and, in extreme cases, coma and death. This is because the brain must have glucose, it cannot use alternative fuels such as lipids.

The *pancreas* is the key organ in the control of blood glucose levels because it makes the hormones insulin and glucagon. Over 90% of the pancreas is dedicated to making pancreatic juice, but there are small patches of cells, the **islets of Langerhans**, that make and secrete hormones (see Fig 20). The islets consist of two types of cells; α (alpha) cells and β (beta) cells. The β cells secrete insulin and the α cells secrete glucagon. These hormones are *antagonistic*; they have opposing effects.

The control of blood glucose is unusual because the central nervous system (CNS) is not directly involved. The α and β cells act as both receptor and effector: they detect changes in glucose levels and they also produce the hormones that reverse the change.

Examiners' Notes

Arterioles are fixed, they can constrict or dilate, but they *do not* 'move to the surface of the skin'.

Arterioles are the only blood vessels that can constrict or dilate. Veins, arteries and capillaries cannot.

Essential Notes

Insulin is a relatively small protein, consisting of 51 amino acids in two polypeptide chains.

Fig 20

The major part of the pancreas makes a juice containing digestive enzymes, but small patches of endocrine cells, the islets of Langerhans, produce the hormones insulin and glucagon

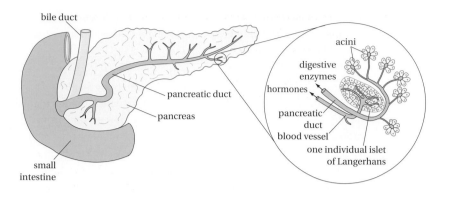

Examiners' Notes

The terms glycogenesis, glycogenolysis and gluconeogenesis look similar and it is easy to confuse them. Look at the key parts of the words: *genesis* = creation, *lysis* = splitting, *neo* = new.

Definition

These definitions are useful for this topic:

Glycogenesis – *the production of* **glycogen** *by the polymerisation of glucose.*

Glycogenolysis – *the breakdown of glycogen to release glucose.*

Gluconeogenesis – *the production of glucose from non-carbohydrate sources (i.e. lipid or protein, but not glycogen). This happens during fasting/dieting/starvation, when glucose and glycogen levels are low.*

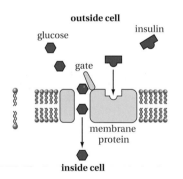

Fig 21

Insulin binds to specific insulin receptor proteins in cell membranes, activating a mechanism that opens extra glucose channels. In this way glucose molecules pass out of the blood and into cells. This process, by definition, is facilitated diffusion

If blood sugar levels are too high ...

Blood glucose levels usually rise for a few hours after a meal, as the sugars and starches are digested into glucose and absorbed into the blood. The high levels are detected by the β cells themselves, which respond by secreting insulin. This hormone travels in the blood and fits into specific receptor proteins on membranes of cells throughout the body, but notably those of the liver.

When insulin fits into the receptor proteins, extra glucose channels open, allowing glucose to pass from the blood into the cells where it can be metabolised (Fig 21). Insulin also activates enzyme pathways that convert glucose into glycogen, protein or lipid.

Type 1 diabetes

Insulin-dependent diabetics, known as type 1 diabetics, cannot make insulin and so glucose cannot pass from blood into cells when needed. Blood glucose levels can then rise – causing hyperglycaemia – while the cells are starved of fuel. Symptoms include:

- **Thirst** – the high glucose levels decrease the water potential of the blood, stimulating the sensation of thirst.

- **Glucose in the urine** – the kidneys normally reabsorb all glucose, but when blood glucose levels are high they are unable to do so.

- **Weight loss** – when starved of their main fuel, cells respire other fuels such as lipids.

- **Breath smells of ketones** (a fruity smell) – ketones are a by-product of lipid metabolism.

- **Excessive urination** – a consequence of the increased fluid intake.

Only about 10%–15% of all diabetics have type 1 diabetes, and it tends to develop in people under the age of 40, often in young children. It is an auto-immune disease in which the body's own immune system destroys the insulin-producing cells. Treatment involves monitoring blood glucose levels, and injections of carefully judged amounts of slow-acting and fast-acting insulin. Each individual learns to manage his or her own condition, recognising early warning symptoms of hyper- or hypoglycaemia, and balancing the diet and exercise with insulin injections.

Type 2 diabetes

This is known as late onset diabetes and is becoming increasingly common due to the high rate of obesity. It is also becoming more common in younger people. Of all diabetics, 85%–90% have type 2 diabetes. The problem is that either the body does not make enough insulin, or that the cells do not respond to it properly. Treatment usually involves a combination of diet, exercise and weight loss.

If blood glucose levels are too low ...

The low levels are detected by the α cells, which respond by secreting glucagon. This peptide hormone travels in the blood and fits into receptor proteins in the same cells that respond to insulin – those that contain stored glycogen. Glucagon acts via a second messenger (see page 11) activating enzyme pathways that break down glycogen. Glucose then passes into the blood, thereby raising blood glucose levels.

3.5.5 Negative feedback helps maintain an optimal internal state in the context of a dynamic equilibrium. Positive feedback also occurs

We have already covered the basics of homeostasis and two important examples: temperature and blood glucose. In this section we look at the control of the oestrus cycle – a more complex example that includes examples of both negative and positive feedback.

There is a hierarchy of control in the oestrus cycle:

- **The hypothalamus** – a region in the brain (see a of Fig 22) that is a vital point of connection between the nervous and hormonal systems. The hypothalamus is sensitive to the levels of many hormones and other physiological factors such as temperature and water potential. It secretes various *releasing factors* that control the many secretions of the pituitary.

- **The pituitary gland** – a key endocrine gland that controls the activities of many other endocrine glands. The pituitary secretes several different hormones (see b of Fig 22) including two that are vital in the oestrus cycle: **FSH** (follicle stimulating hormone) and **LH** (luteinising hormone). Both hormones are classed as *gonadotrophins* (Fig 23). When the hypothalamus secretes a particular *gonadotrophin releasing hormone* (*GnRH*) the pituitary will release either FSH or LH.

- **The gonads** – the primary sex organs: ovaries and testes. Ovaries secrete the steroids oestrogen and progesterone, while the testes secrete testosterone.

In males, a straightforward negative feedback system operates to keep testosterone levels relatively steady. The hypothalamus is sensitive to testosterone levels in the blood. If there is too much the hypothalamus, via the pituitary, will inhibit production. If there is not enough, the hypothalamus will stimulate production.

In females, however, things are more complex. In order to bring about changes such as ovulation, **positive feedbacks** are required.

Fig 22

The position and structure of the hypothalamus and pituitary in the human brain (a) – the hypothalamus is responsible for a wide range of functions, including the control of core temperature and water potential, thirst, hunger, daily rhythms, sexual desire and stress; the pituitary gland secretes several hormones (b)

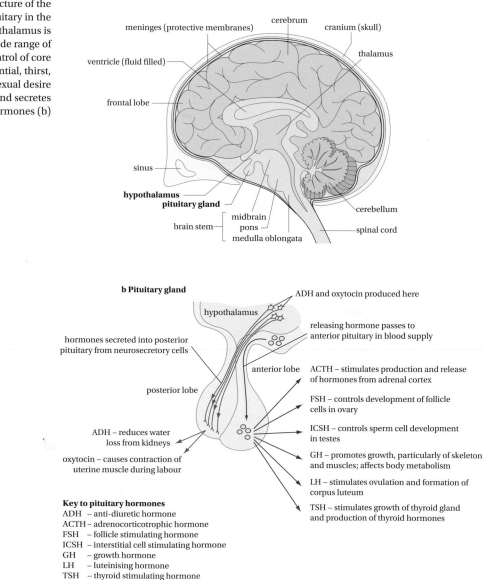

a Cross-section of human brain

- cerebrum
- cranium (skull)
- meninges (protective membranes)
- thalamus
- ventricle (fluid filled)
- frontal lobe
- sinus
- **hypothalamus**
- **pituitary gland**
- cerebellum
- brain stem — midbrain / pons / medulla oblongata
- spinal cord

b Pituitary gland

- hypothalamus
- ADH and oxytocin produced here
- releasing hormone passes to anterior pituitary in blood supply
- hormones secreted into posterior pituitary from neurosecretory cells
- anterior lobe
- ACTH – stimulates production and release of hormones from adrenal cortex
- posterior lobe
- FSH – controls development of follicle cells in ovary
- ICSH – controls sperm cell development in testes
- ADH – reduces water loss from kidneys
- GH – promotes growth, particularly of skeleton and muscles; affects body metabolism
- oxytocin – causes contraction of uterine muscle during labour
- LH – stimulates ovulation and formation of corpus luteum
- TSH – stimulates growth of thyroid gland and production of thyroid hormones

Key to pituitary hormones
ADH – anti-diuretic hormone
ACTH – adrenocorticotrophic hormone
FSH – follicle stimulating hormone
ICSH – interstitial cell stimulating hormone
GH – growth hormone
LH – luteinising hormone
TSH – thyroid stimulating hormone

Control of mammalian oestrus

The oestrus cycle is the reproductive cycle of female mammals. In humans the cycle is usually 25–35 days (typically 28) but it can vary greatly. In females the first cycle happens at puberty and the cycles stop at menopause. The essential features are:

- An **oocyte** (egg cell or ovum) is matured and released during each cycle from one of the ovaries.

- The lining of the uterus is prepared to receive a fertilised embryo.

- If the egg is not fertilised, the lining of the uterus is lost during menstruation and the cycle repeats itself. Menstruation is only seen in primates, not in other mammals.

Examiners' Notes

Exam questions will focus on examples of positive and negative feedback. A negative feedback is a mechanism for stability, reversing any change, while a positive feedback is a mechanism for change.

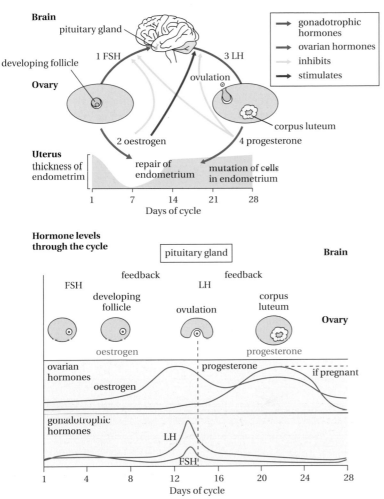

Fig 23
Hormonal control of the menstrual cycle

The events of the menstrual cycle (days relate to Fig 23)

- **Day 1** – beginning of menstruation (a period). The endometrium (uterus lining) comes away. At the same time, the pituitary gland secretes FSH (see Table 3). This stimulates the development of an ovum in the ovary. The ovum becomes surrounded by layers of cells that form a *follicle*. The follicle develops a blood supply, and begins to secrete oestrogen into the blood.

- **Day 5** – menstruation ends when most of the endometrium has been lost but the inner layer remains intact. Oestrogen stimulates mitosis in the endometrium, which begins to thicken again.

- **Days 5–10** – oestrogen levels rise. This inhibits the secretion of the two pituitary hormones, FSH and LH – a negative feedback. The more oestrogen secreted, the more FSH and LH are inhibited (see Table 3).

- **Days 10–14** – in the ovary, oestrogen production by the follicle cells reaches a peak, and the rise of oestrogen level in the blood exerts a *positive* feedback effect. The hypothalamus releases more GnRH, and the responsiveness of the pituitary gland to GnRH increases. The result is a large surge of LH secretion, and a smaller surge of FSH secretion from the pituitary gland. A few hours later the ovum is released from a mature ovarian follicle – the moment of *ovulation* – and the remains of the follicle turn into a *corpus luteum* ('yellow body').

- **Days 15–21** – the corpus luteum begins to secrete progesterone as well as continuing to secrete oestrogen. Progesterone (see Table 3) stimulates the endometrium to mature and become more glandular by secreting specific *glycoproteins* (protein molecules with sugar groups attached). By about Day 21 the endometrium is ready for *implantation* of an embryo.

NB: Progesterone inhibits FSH. This means that no new follicles develop while there is a corpus luteum present in the ovary.

If the egg is not fertilised:

The corpus luteum degenerates and stops secreting progesterone. The inhibition of FSH is lifted, as is the protection that progesterone gave to the endometrium. Menstruation begins and FSH is secreted again, stimulating the development of an ovum.

If the egg is fertilised:

It is essential that the menstrual cycle stops, because menstruation would kill the embryo. To achieve this, the implanted blastocyst gives out a hormone, *human chorionic gonadotrophin* (HCG), that acts as a signal to the corpus luteum to keep secreting progesterone. The detection of HCG is the basis of pregnancy tests.

Table 3
Summary of hormones in the menstrual cycle

Hormone	Type of hormone	Secreted by	Effect(s)
FSH	Gonadotrophin	Anterior pituitary	Stimulates follicle to develop in ovary; helps to stimulate ovulation
Oestrogen	Steroid	Follicle in ovary	Stimulates repair of endometrium
LH	Gonadotrophin	Anterior pituitary	Surge of LH around Day 14 triggers ovulation
Progesterone	Steroid	Corpus luteum in ovary	Stimulates maturation of endometrium; maintains endometrium; inhibits FSH

3.5.6 The sequence of bases in DNA determines the structure of proteins, including enzymes

This section builds on the work covered on DNA structure and replication from AS level Unit 2: *The Variety of Living Organisms*.

The genetic code

The central dogma (idea) of biology is:

$$DNA \rightarrow RNA \rightarrow protein$$

DNA is used to make RNA which, in turn, is used to make proteins. The big question is: **How?**

The genetic code is the sequence of bases in DNA. This sequence codes for the order of amino acids in a polypeptide or protein. A *gene* is a length of DNA that contains all the codons needed to synthesise a particular polypeptide or protein. So how is the genetic code used to build proteins?

There are only four bases (C, A, T and G) but 20 different amino acids, so:

- One base cannot code for one amino acid.

- A two-base code would give $4 \times 4 = 16$ combinations, which is still not enough.

- A three-base code gives $4 \times 4 \times 4 = 64$ possible different combinations, which is more than enough.

> **Definition**
>
> *A group of three bases in DNA or RNA that codes for a particular amino acid is known as a **codon**.*

One codon codes for one amino acid. For example, the codon AAA codes for the amino acid phenylalanine. As there are 64 codons, some amino acids are coded for by more than one. Some codons act as a 'full stop' to stop the amino acid chain growing further.

The genetic code is described as:

- **Universal** – in all organisms the same codons code for the same amino acids.

- **Non–overlapping** – successive codons are read in order, and each nucleotide is part of only one **triplet** codon. For example, the sequence ACTGGA is just two codons, ACT and GGA, not four, as in ACT, CTG, TGG and GGA, because there is no overlap.

- **Degenerate code** – there are more codons than necessary to code for the 20 amino acids. Consequently, some amino acids are coded by several different codons (see Table 4).

Table 4
The mRNA codons that specify particular amino acids

Ala	GCU, GCC, GCA, GCG	Leu	UUA, UUG, CUU, CUC, CUA, CUG
Arg	CGU, CGC, CGA, CGG, AGA, AGG	Lys	AAA, AAG
Asn	AAU, AAC	Met	AUG
Asp	GAU, GAC	Phe	UUU, UUC
Cys	UGU, UGC	Pro	CCU, CCC, CCA, CCG
Gln	CAA, CAG	Ser	UCU, UCC, UCA, UCG, AGU, AGC
Glu	GAA, GAG	Thr	ACU, ACC, ACA, ACG
Gly	GGU, GGC, GGA, GGG	Trp	UGG
His	CAU, CAC	Tyr	UAU, UAC
Ile	AUU, AUC, AUA	Val	GUU, GUC, GUA, GUG
START	AUG	STOP	UAG, UGA, UAA

You will *not* be expected to remember these codons for the exam.

NB: All polypeptide chains are assembled starting with a methionine, which is why the start codon and methionine are the same.

Essential Notes

The hormone insulin, for example, consists of 51 amino acids and so the insulin gene has at least 51 codons, or $51 \times 3 = 153$ bases.

How is the genetic code in DNA used to build a protein? There are two stages:

1 **Transcription**

2 **Translation**.

> **Definition**
>
> *Transcription is the first stage in protein synthesis. The base sequence on a particular gene is copied onto molecules of mRNA (messenger RNA). This takes place in the nucleus.*

The mRNA molecules are effectively mobile copies of genes. They carry the code out of the nucleus to the site of translation, on the **ribosomes** in the cytoplasm.

> **Definition**
>
> *Translation is the second stage in protein synthesis. The base sequence on the mRNA molecule is used to assemble a protein. This takes place on ribosomes.*

Structure of RNA

RNA stands for ribonucleic acid. There are several types of RNA, two of which have a central role in protein synthesis:

- **Messenger RNA (mRNA)** is a single, long strand of nucleotides that is a copy of a gene (Fig 24).

- **Transfer RNA (tRNA)** is a small, cloverleaf-shaped molecule that brings particular amino acids to the ribosome during translation.

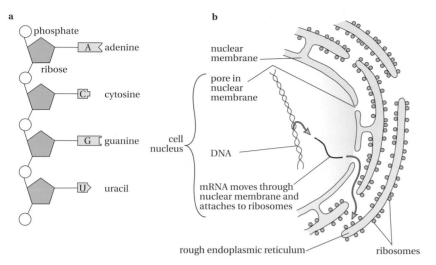

a

phosphate

A adenine

ribose

C cytosine

G guanine

U uracil

b

nuclear membrane

pore in nuclear membrane

cell nucleus

DNA

mRNA moves through nuclear membrane and attaches to ribosomes

rough endoplasmic reticulum

ribosomes

Fig 24
a The structure of a short section of mRNA (messenger RNA)
b Protein synthesis in the cell – transcription happens in the nucleus, while translation happens on the ribosomes

The essential differences between DNA, mRNA and tRNA are summarised in Table 5.

	DNA	mRNA	tRNA
Sugar	Deoxyribose	Ribose	Ribose
Bases	C, G, A and T	C, G, A and U	C, G, A and U
Strands	Double	Single	Single
Shape of molecule	Very long, double helix	Single unfolded strand	Strand folded back on itself, forming a 'clover leaf'
Life span	Long term	Short term	Short term
Site of action	Nucleus	Nucleus and cytoplasm	Cytoplasm

Table 5
A comparison of DNA, mRNA and tRNA. Note that these are RNA codons that have been transcribed from DNA

The process of transcription

Most cells in the human body contain two complete sets of genes. However, only a few genes are used – or *expressed* – in any particular cell. For example, every cell in the human body contains two copies of the gene that codes for insulin, but only certain cells in the pancreas use the gene to make insulin.

The steps in transcription

There are three steps in the process of transcription (Fig 25):

- **Step 1** – the two strands of DNA unwind along the length of the gene. This is catalysed by enzymes.

- **Step 2** – the enzyme **RNA polymerase** moves along one side of the DNA molecule – the *sense strand* that contains the genetic code. The enzyme catalyses the assembly of an mRNA molecule by the addition of matching nucleotides. When RNA is synthesised, the base *thymine* is replaced by *uracil*, so the base pairing in RNA is always A with U and C with G.

- **Step 3** – the mRNA molecule peels off the gene and passes out of the nucleus.

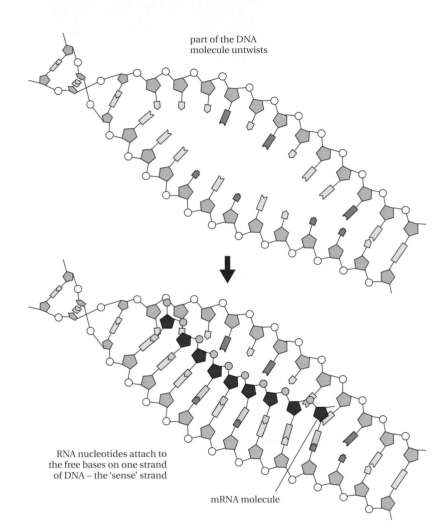

Fig 25
The process of transcription

part of the DNA molecule untwists

RNA nucleotides attach to the free bases on one strand of DNA – the 'sense' strand

mRNA molecule

Introns and exons

In eukaryotic cells, the genes contain DNA sequences that are not used to make the final protein. These sequences are called *introns* and must be spliced (cut) out before translation. The DNA sequences that are going to be expressed are called *exons*.

Following transcription, a molecule of *pre-mRNA* ('pre' is short for 'precursor') exists for a short while, before the introns are spliced out. The resulting *mature mRNA* leaves the nucleus and passes to the ribosomes for translation (Fig 26).

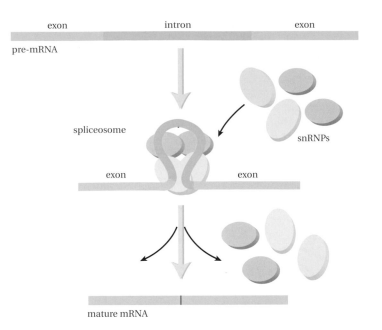

Fig 26
The steps of pre-mRNA splicing (intron removal)
1 The intron loops out as snRNPs (small nuclear ribonucleoprotein particles, complexes of snRNAs and proteins) bind to form the spliceosome
2 The intron is cut out, and the exons are then spliced together
3 The resulting mature mRNA leaves the nucleus to be translated on a ribosome

Translation

Transfer RNA is the molecule that transfers amino acids to ribosomes during translation. It links the genetic code to the protein. At one end of the molecule is the **anticodon** which binds to the codon on the mRNA. At the other end is the amino acid specified by the codon (Fig 27).

A ribosome can be thought of as a giant enzyme that holds together all the components needed for translation (Fig 28):

* **Step 1** – the mRNA attaches itself to a ribosome.

* **Step 2** – the first codon is translated. The first codon is usually AUG, which codes for the amino acid methionine, so a tRNA molecule with the anticodon UAC will attach, carrying a methionine molecule at the other end.

* **Step 3** – the second codon is translated in the same way. The second amino acid is held alongside the first, and a peptide bond is formed by condensation between them. The polypeptide chain has started. ATP is split to provide the energy to form the peptide bond.

* **Step 4** – the process is repeated – the mRNA moves along the ribosome until the polypeptide has been built. If a stop codon is encountered, translation ceases and the polypeptide is finished.

Once the protein/polypeptide has been assembled, it folds and bends into its tertiary structure and accumulates on the inside of the rough endoplasmic reticulum. Here it is packaged into vesicles (spheres of membrane) and may pass to the Golgi apparatus where it is modified and/or activated. Some proteins are used inside the cells, and some are for export in which case they leave the cell by exocytosis.

Fig 27
The structure of transfer RNA (tRNA)

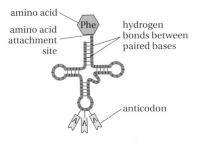

Examiners' Notes

Do not describe a ribosome as an enzyme in an exam; strictly speaking it is not.

The problems you will be given usually involve both transcription and translation, and will test whether you realise that A in DNA is transcribed into U in mRNA and that the corresponding base in tRNA is A. Make a revision list similar to this for all four bases.

You might also be asked this in reverse, for example, 'What base on DNA is represented by U in tRNA?'

Fig 28
The overall process of translation

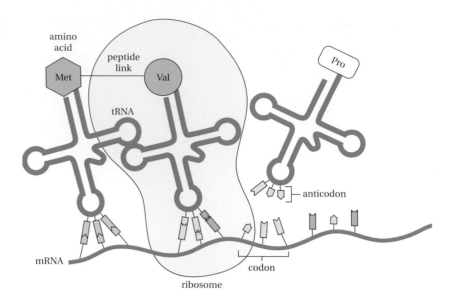

Gene mutation

Essential Notes

This section deals only with *gene* **mutations**. There are also chromosome mutations that involve fragments of chromosomes – whole blocks of genes – being lost or duplicated. Think of gene mutations as putting the wrong word into a book, while a chromosome mutation is the loss of a whole chapter.

A gene mutation occurs when there is a change in the sequence of bases, such as when a gene is copied incorrectly. This can result in one or more incorrect amino acids being incorporated into the protein. For example, if a codon that read AAA was copied incorrectly so that it read AAC, then asparagine would replace lysine (look back at Table 4).

Gene mutation can happen in three different ways:

- substitution (or point mutation)
- addition
- deletion.

Substitution is where the wrong base is inserted.

For example, consider the base sequence:

> AAT CGG CCC GTA

This will be transcribed into mRNA as:

> UUA GCC GGG CAU

and then translated into the amino acid sequence:

> leucine–alanine–glycine–histidine

If one base is substituted, so that the DNA sequence now reads:

> AAT C<u>A</u>G CCC GTA

the second codon will be transcribed as GUC which translates into the amino acid valine. So valine will replace alanine in the amino acid chain. This change to the primary structure of the protein might or might not affect the way the polypeptide chain folds and bends to produce the tertiary structure. If the new amino acid significantly changes the tertiary and/or quaternary structure (that is, the overall shape) the protein might not be able to function properly.

Addition is when an extra base is added into the sequence. All the bases that follow in the sequence are moved along. This is known as a **frame shift**. Addition could cause the sequence:

ATT CGG CCC GTA

to become:

AT<u>C</u> TCG GCC CGT

This will cause most of the amino acids coded for by codons at or after the addition to change.

A **deletion** involves the loss of a base, causing a frame shift in the other direction as all the bases move along to replace the one that was lost. This will also change most of the codons at or after the deletion. Overall, additions and deletions are more disruptive than substitutions.

Gene mutations can have one of three consequences:

- **They might be lethal**. The new amino acid causes the protein to be significantly different to the original, so that it does not perform its function in the organism (see Table 6). For instance, it might mean that the active site of an enzyme is the wrong shape to combine with the substrate. This might result in a *metabolic block*, in which the enzyme cannot play its part in a sequence of reactions, so that essential products are in short supply while intermediate compounds build up. Mutations that cause frame shifts are more likely to be lethal than substitutions because they change more codons, and thus more amino acids. A protein is more likely to function with one amino acid change than with a whole new sequence.

- **They might have no effect**. The protein might still function despite the new amino acid because the change does not alter the tertiary structure or the shape of the part of the protein which interacts with other chemicals. Also, because some amino acids are coded for by several different codons, a mutation might not result in a change in the amino acid.

- **They might be beneficial**. The new amino acid might alter the protein in such a way that it works in a different way – one that helps the organism. This will confer a *selective advantage* on the individual. Individuals that have a selective advantage are more likely to survive and reproduce, passing their alleles or allele combinations on to the next generation.

A classic example of a beneficial mutation is seen in the peppered moth. The speckled variety of this moth was common in the UK before the time of the Industrial Revolution. Its speckled coloration gave it camouflage on light-coloured, lichen-covered rocks and tree bark. However, the industrial processes of the Industrial Revolution covered many surfaces with a layer of soot – the speckled moths stood out and were seen more easily by predators. A chance mutation in a gene (not *caused* by the soot) created an allele that caused a change in colouration, producing a black (melanic) variety of moth. The mutants were better camouflaged on sooty surfaces and so had a selective advantage. With every generation, the frequency of the melanic allele increased, and the melanic form became more common in sooty areas than the speckled form.

What causes mutations?

Mutations normally occur by chance, just random mistakes in the copying of DNA, although the rate of mutation can be greatly increased by **mutagens.** These include:

- ultraviolet light
- X-rays
- α and β radiation
- chemicals such as mustard gas and cigarette smoke.

Table 6 lists some examples of lethal gene mutations.

Examiners' Notes

Do not fall into the classic error of stating that all mutations are harmful.

Table 6
Examples of lethal gene mutations

Disease	Function of healthy allele	Consequence of mutant allele
Cystic fibrosis	CFTR gene codes for a protein that transports ions across lung membranes, leading to normal watery mucus	No ion transport, so mucus becomes thick and sticky; lungs are easily infected
Haemophilia	Codes for Factor VIII, an essential protein in the chain reaction leading to blood clotting	Leads to a fault in the blood-clotting mechanism; even minor cuts lead to major blood loss
Phenylketonuria (PKU)	Codes for an enzyme that converts the amino acid phenylalanine into tyrosine	An example of a lethal metabolic block – phenylalanine and other related substances build up, interfering with brain development in the baby

Gene mutations and cancer

Usually, cells in the human body only divide when they should, in order to allow growth or the repair of tissues. When the mechanisms that control cell division (mitosis) break down, the result is the uncontrolled division of cells, resulting in a tumour (Fig 29).

There are two types of tumours:

- **Benign** – these tumours are enclosed in a capsule and grow in the centre, so they do not invade the surrounding tissues; they are not cancerous and are often easily removed by surgery.

- **Malignant** – these tumours grow at the edges, invading the surrounding tissues and organs; they are cancerous and are much more difficult to treat. Often it is difficult to tell where their boundaries are, making surgery difficult. Cells can break off and set up secondary tumours elsewhere in the body – this spreading process is called metastasis, as shown in Fig 29.

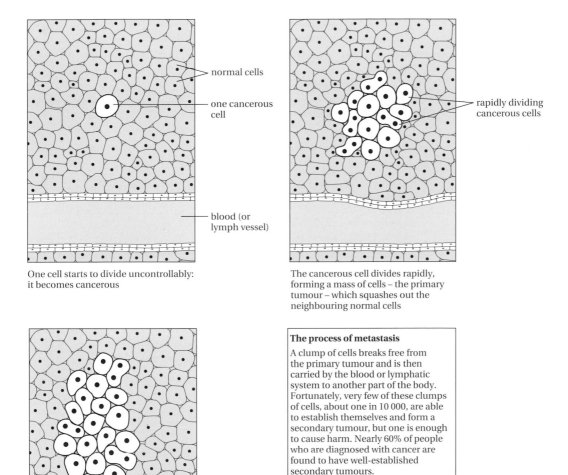

One cell starts to divide uncontrollably: it becomes cancerous

The cancerous cell divides rapidly, forming a mass of cells – the primary tumour – which squashes out the neighbouring normal cells

The process of metastasis
A clump of cells breaks free from the primary tumour and is then carried by the blood or lymphatic system to another part of the body. Fortunately, very few of these clumps of cells, about one in 10 000, are able to establish themselves and form a secondary tumour, but one is enough to cause harm. Nearly 60% of people who are diagnosed with cancer are found to have well-established secondary tumours.

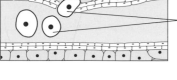

Fig 29
The development of a tumour and the process of metastasis

The causes of cancer

There are many factors involved in the development of cancer, including genetic and environmental factors, as described overleaf.

Genetic factors

The development of cancer can be caused by a mutation of the genes that control cell division. Scientists have isolated several **proto-oncogenes**. When these mutate into **oncogenes** the cell loses its ability to control cell division.

The incidence of cancer, however, is much rarer than the mutation of oncogenes. This is because there is a back-up control system in the form of *tumour suppressor genes*. These genes prevent cells from dividing too quickly, giving time for the immune system to destroy the rogue cells, or for the damaged DNA to be repaired. If the tumour suppressor genes mutate, the cell's safety mechanisms are lost, and the development of cancer is more likely.

Cancer is more common in older people because their somatic (body) cells accumulate mutations. Sometimes, however, these mutations occur in gametes (sex cells), so that the genes are passed on to the next generation. People who inherit these genes are said to have a genetic predisposition to cancer; that is, they are more likely to develop cancer, especially at an early age.

Environmental factors

There are many factors that increase the rate of mutation of the cells described above, and so increase the risk of developing cancer. Such factors are called **carcinogens** and include:

- **Smoking** – tobacco smoke contains a variety of carcinogens.

- **Diet** – several substances we eat or drink can cause cancer, for example, alcohol has been linked with a higher incidence of mouth, throat and oesophageal cancer. A lack of fibre and a high intake of red meat and animal fat seems to be associated with cancers of the colon and rectum, which are very common in the Western world.

- **Radiation** – certain types of radiation are known to be carcinogenic because they damage DNA. Ultraviolet radiation (in sunlight) does not penetrate far into human tissue but it can cause skin cancer. Ionising radiation, for example, from nuclear fallout, can penetrate much further and can cause cancers such as leukaemia (cancer of the bone marrow).

- **Chemical carcinogens** – asbestos, benzene, methanal (formaldehyde) and diesel exhaust fumes are all carcinogenic.

- **Microorganisms** – viruses, in particular, have been linked with the development of cancers. The *human papilloma virus* (*HPV*) is associated with over 90% of cases of cervical cancer.

3.5.7 Gene expression is controlled by a number of features

Most of a cell's DNA is not translated

Multicellular organisms such as humans start out life as one fertilised egg – a zygote. Looking at the genome of that cell (Fig 30), it is apparent that the genes only form a small amount of the total DNA. Most of the DNA is found between the genes and is known as *non-coding DNA*. This is never transcribed or translated. It has been estimated that between 1%–2% of the human genome

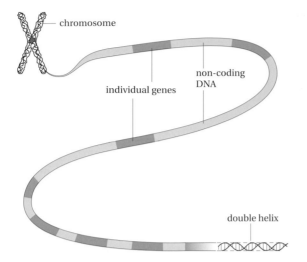

Fig 30
There is a lot of non-coding DNA between the genes, and some – the introns – are found within genes. Generally, the more complex the organism, the greater the percentage of non-coding DNA in the genome

actually codes for proteins. The rest has been described as junk DNA but it might have an important function in the expression of the coding sequences.

How does a single-celled embryo grow and develop into a complex, organised individual such as a human? We know that the secret lies in the control of *cell division* and *cell differentiation*. Cells know when to divide and when to remain in interphase. We also know that cells differentiate, or specialise, by the selective activation of certain genes. Cells that have the potential to differentiate into different specialised cells are called **stem cells**.

Different types of stem cells

Stem cells have two key properties:

1 **Self-renewal** – the ability to go through numerous cycles of mitosis while remaining undifferentiated.

2 **Potency** – the capacity to differentiate into specialised cell types.

Broadly, stem cells come from two sources; *embryos* and *adults*. Generally, adult stem cells are more limited in their potency than embryonic stem cells.

In terms of potency, there are three broad types:

1 **Totipotent** stem cells have the potential to differentiate into any of the 216 or so known cell types that make up the human body. The early embryo (more accurately, the blastocyst) contains totipotent stem cells, but the use of embryos is controversial (see page 44).

2 **Pluripotent** stem cells are the descendents of totipotent cells and are found in certain adult tissues such as blood from the umbilical cord. They also have the potential to differentiate into a wide variety of cell types.

3 **Multipotent** stem cells have limited potential, and can just differentiate into a few closely related cell types. For example, *haematopoietic stem cells* in bone marrow can differentiate into red blood cells, different types of white blood cells and platelets. Most adult stem cells are multipotent.

In contrast to animals, many plant cells remain totipotent even when apparently specialised in the adult. Many students will be familiar with the practical technique of **cloning** a whole new plant from an already-specialised piece of tissue, such as a leaf or a root.

Micropropagation

The totipotency of adult plant cells is put to good use in micropropagation, a technique that clones large numbers of plants in a relatively short time.

The process involves taking a small piece of the plant to be cloned – called the *explant* – and ensuring that it is sterile (free from bacteria and viruses). The explant is then grown in ideal conditions (humidity, temperature, nutrients) and a culture medium that may include particular hormones. The explant can be divided again and again, producing hundreds or thousands of new ones. Complete new plants will develop from each explant, though each must be 'hardened off' before it will be ready to withstand harsher conditions in greenhouses or outside.

Advantages of micropropagation include:

- rapidly produces large numbers of identical, disease-free plants
- does not take up much space – can be done on a tabletop
- it is the only way to produce some species such as orchids, genetically modified plants, or seedless varieties.

Disadvantages of micropropagation include:

- does not work for all plants
- if the original explant is infected, all the new plants will be too
- very labour intensive.

The potential of stem cells

Stem cell research is still in its infancy, but many people believe that is has enormous potential in science and medicine. The treatment of leukaemia with a bone marrow transplant is a well-established technique but there are many more possibilities, for example:

- making new skin for burns victims, or people with skin ulcers
- making pancreatic cells for diabetics
- repairing spinal cord injuries and other nerve damage
- repairing muscle damage, for example, after a heart attack
- making certain brain cells for sufferers of Alzheimer's and Parkinson's disease.

There is also a wider goal: the study of stem cells can lead to a better understanding of how organisms grow and develop, and could shed more light on the mechanisms behind cellular control and why it sometimes goes wrong, as in the case of tumour development (see page 40, on cancer).

The ethics of stem cell research

There is a great deal of controversy over human embryonic stem cell research. One key reason is that starting a new stem cell line requires the destruction of a human embryo.

Opponents of the research argue that embryonic stem cell technology is a slippery slope to reproductive cloning (i.e. of a whole individual) and that it can fundamentally devalue human life. Those in the pro-life movement argue that a human embryo is a human life and is therefore entitled to protection.

On the other hand, supporters of embryonic stem cell research argue that it should be pursued because of the potential to relieve suffering (see 'The potential of stem cells'). It is also true that excess embryos created in IVF (*in vitro* fertilisation) programmes for infertility could be donated with consent and used for the research. They argue that the embryo is a piece of tissue, not an individual with a nervous system, and if the people who created it are willing to donate it, there is no suffering or loss to anyone.

The regulation of transcription and translation

How are some genes switched on while others remain dormant? **Transcription** of a specific gene is only possible when a number of *transcription factors* are in place. The control of transcription is the key to the selective activation of genes. A gene is switched on, or *induced*, when transcription begins.

Transcription starts when the enzyme RNA polymerase and several proteins (known as transcription) factors bind to an area adjacent to the gene, called the *promoter region*. The proteins assemble into a *transcription initiation complex* (*TIC*). Once this complex is in place, transcription can begin (Fig 31).

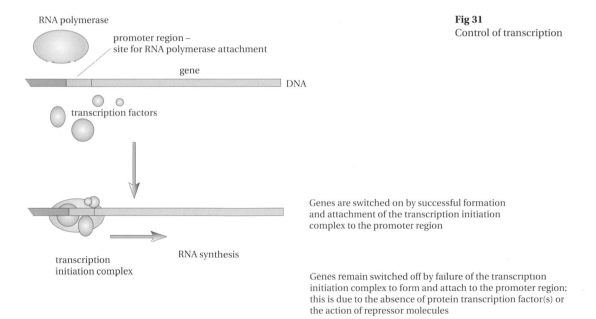

Fig 31
Control of transcription

Genes are switched on by successful formation and attachment of the transcription initiation complex to the promoter region

Genes remain switched off by failure of the transcription initiation complex to form and attach to the promoter region; this is due to the absence of protein transcription factor(s) or the action of repressor molecules

Some transcription factors are always present in a cell, some are present but in an inactive form, and some are not made until a key stage in a cell's life. Genes remain switched off until the correct transcription factors are present, and in their active form. Transcription factors can be activated by *signal proteins*, which may be **hormones,** *growth factors* or other regulatory molecules.

In addition, transcription can be prevented by the presence of certain repressor molecules which attach to the promotor region and prevent the formation of the TIC.

Pioneering work on gene induction was done by Jacob and Monod in the early 1960s. They worked on the bacterium *E. coli*.

E. coli can digest lactose (milk sugar) by making the enzyme β galactosidase. When there is no lactose, the enzyme is not made because the β galactosidase gene is not active. However, the presence of lactose causes the gene to be induced. Jacob and Monod found that in the absence of lactose there was a repressor molecule that bound to the promotor region and prevented the formation of the TIC. When lactose was present, the repressor molecule was removed and the gene was activated.

The role of oestrogen in gene transcription

Oestrogen is a steroid, a lipid hormone that passes through the cell surface membrane, through the cytoplasm and into the nucleus. Oestrogen binds with and activates nuclear **oestrogen** receptors (known as ERs – from the American spelling *estrogen*).

The main function of these intracellular oestrogen receptors is as transcription factors which bind to DNA, thus regulating gene expression and stimulating the cell to make specific proteins.

siRNA

A new class of RNA molecules has recently been found that has a variety of functions in the cell, including the control of transcription. That is, they can act as *repressor molecules*. Called **small interfering RNA** (**siRNA**) they form a class of small molecules, 20–25 nucleotides long and double stranded. Most notably, siRNA is involved in the RNA interference (RNAi) pathway where the siRNA interferes with the expression of a specific gene.

siRNAs have great potential in medicine and genetic engineering, because they can be made artificially and introduced into cells to bring about the specific *knockdown* of a particular gene, for example, one that causes a particular type of cancer. In theory, any gene for which the sequence is known can be de-activated by a tailor-made siRNA molecule.

3.5.8 Gene cloning technologies allow study and alteration of gene function in order to better understand organism function and to design new industrial and medical processes

In recent years we have progressed from the study of genes and genetics to taking a more active role. We now have the ability to identify genes and find out what they do. We can also cut them out, copy them and insert them into other organisms. There are many potential applications, including:

- enhancing an effect already natural to that organism (for example, to increase growth rate)

- increasing resistance to disease or damage (for example, for crops – blight, cold or drought)

- repairing a genetic 'defect' – the process of gene therapy
- enabling an organism to synthesise something it would not normally make; for example, genetically modifying animals, plants or microorganisms to produce proteins for use in human medicine.

A common process in genetic engineering is to isolate a gene that codes for a useful product and transfer the gene into a microorganism such as bacteria or yeast. These organisms can be cultured easily, they grow rapidly and they can express the gene and make large amounts of the valuable product. Examples of products made in this way include human insulin and other human hormones, antibiotics and enzymes.

Transgenic organisms have had their DNA altered by the insertion of genes from another organism. For example, some cereal crops have had genes for disease resistance inserted. Most of our genetically modified foods have had beneficial genes inserted into their genome (a source of heated debate).

Transgenic organisms contain *recombinant DNA*, which is DNA that has been mixed with that of another species. Usually the entire genome of a transgenic organism is intact, it has simply had one or two specific genes added. For example, Dolly, the cloned sheep is still a sheep, even with a human gene added. She is not a Frankenstein sheep, despite what the media may report.

Gene cloning and transfer

Once a useful gene or DNA sequence has been found, there are several ways to isolate it, including:

- working backwards from mRNA; the enzyme **reverse transcriptase** can make a piece of **complementary DNA (cDNA)** from mature mRNA
- cutting it out of the chromosome using enzymes called **restriction endonucleases**.

Restriction enzymes and ligases

Restriction endonucleases – more commonly called restriction enzymes – originate in bacteria where their function is to protect against viral attack by cutting viral DNA. There are hundreds of different restriction enzymes currently available.

A particular restriction enzyme will cut DNA at a specific **recognition site**. These sites are typically between four and eight nucleotides long and many of them are **palindromic sequences**, meaning that the sequence on one strand reads the same as the corresponding sequence on the complementary strand when read in the reverse direction (Fig 32). The meaning of 'palindromic' in this context is different from its linguistic usage: GTAATG is not a palindromic DNA sequence, but GTATAC is (GTATAC is *complementary* to CATATG).

The cuts made in the DNA are often staggered, so that one strand is several bases longer than the other (Fig 33). These are known as **sticky ends**.

Another enzyme, DNA **ligase**, can be used to join pieces of DNA that have been cut by the same restriction enzyme and therefore have complementary sticky ends. Think of restriction and ligase enzymes as molecular scissors and glue, but do not use this description in the exam.

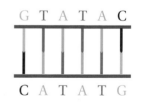

Fig 32
A palindromic recognition site reads the same on the reverse strand as it does on the forward strand – simply read from the other end

Fig 33
Some restriction enzymes make staggered cuts, rather than clean ones, so that a few bases are exposed – four in this example; this allows the cut to be connected to any other piece of DNA that has been cut with the same enzyme. Note that the recognition site is palindromic

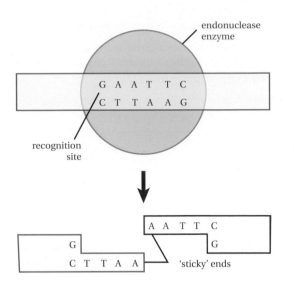

Once found, the useful gene or DNA fragment can be copied in one of two ways (Table 7 on page 50 lists the advantages and disadvantages of each):

- ***in vivo*** ('in life' – using living cells) or

- ***in vitro*** ('in glass' – gene cloning in a test tube is achieved simply and quickly by the process of **PCR** – the polymerase chain reaction).

In vivo cloning

This technique involves putting the desired piece of DNA into a **vector** such as a plasmid or virus, and then using the vector to 'smuggle' the DNA into a host cell such as a bacterium. The host cell will (sometimes) adopt the new DNA and express it to make a particular protein (Fig 34).

Fig 34
The process of *in vivo* cloning

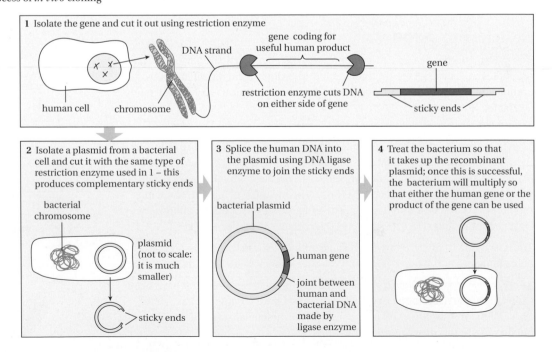

One example of this is the manufacture of human insulin. The human insulin gene is isolated and multiple copies are made, using PCR. Then the gene must be inserted into a bacterium, which is achieved using plasmids as vectors.

The problem with this process is its unreliability. When plasmids are mixed with bacteria, for every bacterium that takes up a plasmid, tens of thousands do not. So how do you tell which bacteria have accepted the new gene? One way is to add a *genetic marker* – an extra gene inserted into the plasmid along with the gene that is to be cloned.

A common example of a genetic marker is a gene for antibiotic resistance. In a technique called *replica plating*, the bacteria are then grown on a medium that contains the antibiotic. Only those bacteria that took up the plasmid with the new gene and the gene for antibiotic resistance will survive and grow. Another example of a genetic marker is a gene which makes an enzyme that makes a coloured product. The bacteria are then grown with the required substrate in the growth medium, and any transgenic colonies will show up and so are easily seen and collected.

In vitro cloning (PCR)

DNA cloning in a test tube is done by the process of PCR. Starting with a tiny sample of DNA, PCR can make millions of copies within about an hour.

The ingredients needed are:

- the original DNA sample
- nucleotides
- **DNA polymerase** enzyme
- primers – short sequences of nucleotides that 'show' the polymerase enzyme where to start.

The basic steps of DNA cloning in a test tube are as shown in Fig 35.

Essential Notes

Plasmids are small circles of DNA that are found in bacterial cytoplasm.

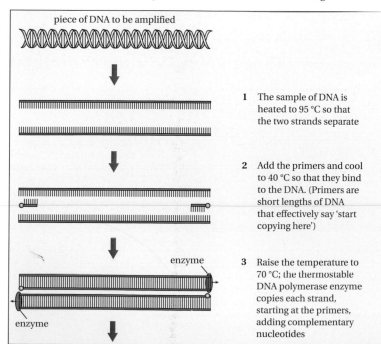

piece of DNA to be amplified

1   The sample of DNA is heated to 95 °C so that the two strands separate

2   Add the primers and cool to 40 °C so that they bind to the DNA. (Primers are short lengths of DNA that effectively say 'start copying here')

enzyme

3   Raise the temperature to 70 °C; the thermostable DNA polymerase enzyme copies each strand, starting at the primers, adding complementary nucleotides

enzyme

Fig 35
The essential stages in PCR

One cycle of the chain reaction takes a couple of minutes, so if repeated continuously, you can easily get over a million copies within an hour. There are sophisticated PCR machines that automate the whole process.

Essential Notes

Thermostable enzymes work at high temperatures without being denatured.

It is essential that the DNA polymerase enzyme used in PCR is thermostable, so that it can be added to the mixture at the start and will not be denatured by the temperatures used. Many PCR applications use **Taq polymerase**, an enzyme originally isolated from the thermophilic ('heat loving') bacterium *Thermus aquaticus*.

The polymerase chain reaction has many uses. For example, tiny DNA samples taken at a crime scene can be copied quickly to give enough DNA for forensic analysis. It can also be used in *genetic screening* as it allows scientists to take a tiny sample of tissue and multiply the DNA until there is enough to test for the presence of a particular disease. For example, in this way we can test for the presence of the cystic fibrosis gene from just a sample of saliva.

Table 7
The relative advantages of *in vivo* and *in vitro* cloning

	In vivo (in organism)	*In vitro* (using PCR)
Advantages	Gene can be expressed (used to make protein); proofreading enzymes correct copying mistakes	Very quick; little purification of final sample needed
Disadvantages	Relatively slow, with more complex purification	Mistakes in copying the base sequence are common

Table 8
Some current issues in gene technology

The pros and cons of DNA technology

Activity	Possible objection
Inserting human genes into other animals, for example, sheep, so that the gene is expressed and the product can be purified from the milk	Unknown long-term effects of interfering with a complex organism's genome
Inserting human genes into microorganisms, for culturing on an industrial scale	Who 'owns' the product – the company that makes it or the original source?
Transferring beneficial genes into plants	Possible danger when interfering with an organism's genome is that it may have unexpected effects, for example, toxic by-products, effects on the ecosystem; horizontal gene transfer – genes can be swapped between plant species
Using embryos for research	When does an embryo become a human being, with its own rights?
Cloning organisms; for example, embryos of prize cattle can be split many times to produce identical embryos which can be implanted into ordinary cattle	Slippery slope to cloning humans – possible psychological problems. Should a person be allowed to clone themselves for reasons of vanity?
Animal organs for human transplant	Concerns about safety; the 'yuk' factor (instinctive revulsion); some claim that it is 'speciesist' – it implies that humans are superior to other species, when morally we should grant all species equal rights

Any development could be evaluated against the following criteria:

1 **Technical difficulty** – is the activity too difficult (or expensive) to do reliably?

2 **Ethical problems** – human issues. Is the activity immoral?

3 **Potential catastrophe** – something unknown could happen. Can we predict all possible outcomes of the development?

Criterion 1 for any development will probably diminish with time as practical techniques and methods improve. Criterion 3 will also change as techniques and methods change; we should get better at prediction. Criterion 2, however, will always be an issue (as Table 8 on the previous page shows).

Gene therapy

Gene therapy is the treatment of genetic disease by replacing defective alleles with functional allelles. It sounds simple in theory. The basic steps are:

- Isolate the allele that is causing the disease.

- Work out the base sequence of the healthy allele.

- Make lots of copies of the healthy allele (that is, clone it).

- Deliver it into the cells/tissues in which the defective allele is being expressed.

In practice, though, there are many difficulties to be overcome and this line of treatment is still in its infancy; however, it does have great potential. A lot of research has focused on the liver, which has a high metabolic activity. Many diseases are associated with the inability to make a particular liver enzyme.

One such disease is GSD 1a (glycogen storage disease type 1a). Sufferers cannot make the enzyme glucose-6-phosphatase and consequently cannot break down glycogen. This means that blood glucose levels can fall dangerously low and sufferers need to eat large amounts of starch so that the slow release of glucose keeps levels up.

Trials have taken place recently in which healthy copies of the gene that codes for glucose-6-phosphatase have been inserted into viruses (specifically, adenoviruses). These viruses have been made to target liver cells, but they should not cause disease and cannot reproduce. The virus introduces the gene into the liver cells, where it is expressed and used to make the working enzyme. Results have been very encouraging so far, but it will be a while before such treatment is widely available.

Medical diagnosis

As our knowledge of the human genome increases, we are finding more and more genes that predispose individuals to certain diseases, such as prostate cancer or coronary heart disease. This increases the demand for screening and treatment.

How do we find out whether an individual has inherited a particular gene or allele? One way is to use a genetic probe. This is a small piece of DNA that can be used to test an individual for a particular gene, such as one that causes a disease. The probe is complementary to a short base sequence on the gene of interest, and has a fluorescent or radioactive label. When added to the sample of DNA, the probe will seek out and bind to the gene, showing its presence.

Restriction mapping

Restriction mapping is the process of locating the restriction sites in a piece of DNA. This is done by using restriction enzymes, and analysing the resulting fragments (Fig 36).

Restriction map information is important for many techniques in DNA analysis and manipulation. One application is to cut a large piece of DNA into smaller fragments to allow it to be sequenced. Genes and cDNAs can be thousands of kilobases long, but they can only be sequenced 400 bases at a time. DNA must be chopped into smaller pieces and cloned again ('subcloned') to perform the sequencing.

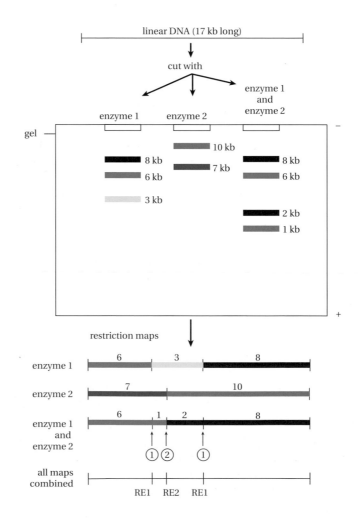

Fig 36
A simple example of restriction mapping; we want to map this length of DNA, which is 17 kilobases (17 000) bases long

1 If we cut it with restriction enzyme 1, and separate the fragments by electrophoresis, we get three fragments: 8, 6 and 3 kb long; this tells us that the restriction site for this enzyme appears *twice* in our fragment

2 If we 'digest' with enzyme 2, we get fragments of 10 and 7, so there is only *one* restriction site for enzyme 2, and it must be 7 kb from one end and 10 kb from the other

3 If we digest with both enzymes, we get our original 8 and 6 kb fragments and new ones of 2 and 1 kb; this tells us that the restriction site for enzyme 2 must be in the 3 kb fragment

Putting all this information together, we can produce a restriction map of our piece of DNA

DNA sequencing

The base sequence of a piece of DNA is most commonly worked out using **dideoxy sequencing**. This is a major technique – it was used to sequence the entire human genome, all three billion base pairs.

The ingredients

- the original piece of DNA – just a single strand
- primers, radioactively or fluorescently labelled
- DNA polymerase
- normal nucleotides (consisting of sugar, phosphate and C, A, T or G)
- special nucleotides that stop the polymerase enzyme from adding any more bases; these are called dideoxynucleotides, or ddNTPs for short; specifically, these are ddATP, ddGTP, ddCTP, or ddTTP.

The process

The DNA sample is divided into four separate tubes, each containing:

- the four labelled nucleotides (written as dATP, dGTP, dCTP and dTTP)
- DNA polymerase
- primers
- only one of the four dideoxynucleotides (ddATP, ddGTP, ddCTP, or ddTTP); the normal nucleotides should form about 99% of the reaction mixture, with only 1% ddNTPs.

The reaction will proceed, just like PCR, until the enzyme tries to add one of the special (dd) nucleotides. Then it stops. So, for instance, in the tube that contains ddGTP, *we know that every fragment of DNA will finish with the base G.* There are approximately 100 times more normal nucleotides than dd nucleotides, but by the law of averages every G nucleotide will become the end of the chain in some fragments.

NB: Sometimes the primers have the radioactive or fluorescent marker, sometimes it is the ddNTPs. It does not really matter which has the marker; both will allow the fragments to show up after electrophoresis.

So how do you figure out the base sequence?

The newly synthesised and labelled DNA fragments are double stranded, so they are denatured by heat and separated by size (with a resolution of just one nucleotide) by gel electrophoresis on a special gel. Each of the four DNA synthesis reactions is run in one of four individual lanes – one from each tube. The DNA bands are then made visible by autoradiography or UV light, and the DNA sequence can be directly read off the X-ray film or gel image.

Looking at the sample (Fig 37), we can see that the smallest fragment (that is, the one that travelled furthest down the gel) was in the T lane, so T is the first base in the sequence. Then it is A, followed by T, G and G. This is the complementary sequence to the original piece of DNA.

Fig 37

The dideoxy sequencing method. The smallest fragments move more quickly through the gel: the smallest fragment, which must be a single nucleotide, is a T; the next smallest fragment, which is only two bases long, ends with an A; then it is T, G, G and so on. Note that the sequence on the newly synthesised strand is *complementary* to the original strand; once you know the sequence of the complementary strand, it is easy to work out the original sequence

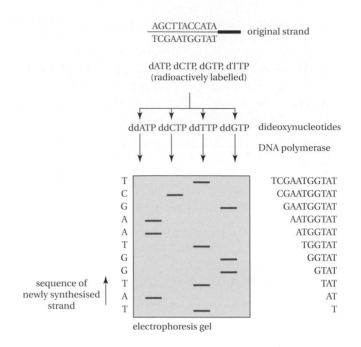

DNA fingerprinting

This technique – more accurately called DNA profiling – was developed at Leicester University by Alec Jeffreys in 1984. It is proving to be an invaluable tool in forensic medicine and has many other applications.

The principles

Within the non-coding DNA are *hypervariable regions*, so called because they vary enormously in length from person to person. These regions consist of

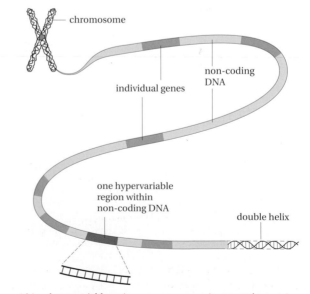

Fig 38

Although each chromosome contains hundreds or thousands of genes, they only account for a small proportion of the length: over 95% is non-coding DNA; within these segments are hypervariable regions. These are unique to each individual and, when they are separated, the pattern they form provides the basis of DNA profiling

within a hypervariable region a core sequence is repeated a certain number of times: different people have different numbers of repeats and therefore different-sized hypervariable regions

particular base sequences which are repeated again and again. They are classed as *minisatellites* (about 10–100 base pairs), and *microsatellites* (mostly 2–4 base pairs). Different people have different numbers of repeats and so have differently sized hypervariable regions. When these are labelled and separated according to size, a pattern is produced. Each pattern is unique to each individual person and can be used as the basis of DNA profiling (Fig 39).

Getting a sample of DNA

All body cells contain the same DNA, and so virtually any tissue sample can be used for DNA profiling. Thanks to PCR (page 49) the amount of tissue required is very small: 0.05 cm^3 of blood, 0.005 cm^3 of semen or one hair root. Semen contains more DNA than blood because red cells have no nucleus. Only the white cells in blood yield any useful DNA.

Processing the DNA and separating the fragments

Once you have a DNA sample, the next stage is to cut the molecule using restriction enzymes (see page 47). The result is a mixture of DNA fragments, some of which contain the hypervariable regions.

Electrophoresis separates the fragments according to electrical charge or size. The fragment mixture is placed in a well in some gel. The DNA is negatively charged because it contains phosphate groups. When a current is applied, the DNA fragments move towards the positive terminal, or anode. The gel is essentially a mesh of long polymer molecules, and smaller DNA fragments can squeeze through the gaps more easily than the larger ones. The fragments separate into bands (Fig 40) according to size – the smaller the fragment, the faster it moves through the gel.

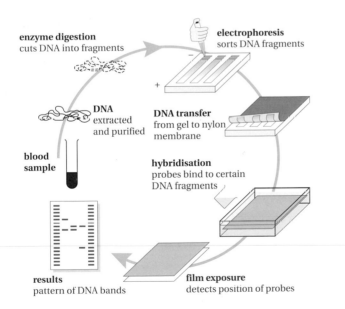

enzyme digestion
cuts DNA into fragments

electrophoresis
sorts DNA fragments

DNA
extracted
and purified

DNA transfer
from gel to nylon
membrane

blood
sample

hybridisation
probes bind to certain
DNA fragments

results
pattern of DNA bands

film exposure
detects position of probes

Fig 39
The major steps in the preparation of a DNA profile

The bands of DNA are transferred from the gel onto a nylon membrane by *Southern blotting*, a process that works by capillary action. At this stage the bands are still invisible. They must be stained so that the hypervariable regions can be seen.

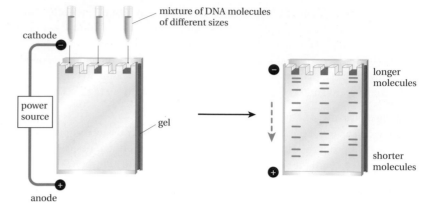

Fig 40
Electrophoresis

Labelling the fragments

Within hypervariable regions are core sequences that are common to all humans. It is the number of times the sequences are repeated that varies from person to person.

Pieces of DNA complementary to these core sequences have been isolated and are produced in bulk for use as genetic probes. They are labelled with a marker chemical, commonly the enzyme alkaline phosphatase which fluoresces (produces light) when a particular substrate is added.

When the probes, complete with enzyme, are added to the DNA sample, they attach to the core sequences, thus marking the hypervariable regions. Excess probe is washed off, substrate for the enzyme is added, and bands that contain hypervariable regions fluoresce. If the blot is exposed to an X-ray film, dark lines appear wherever bands in the blot have emitted light, forming the familiar DNA profile.

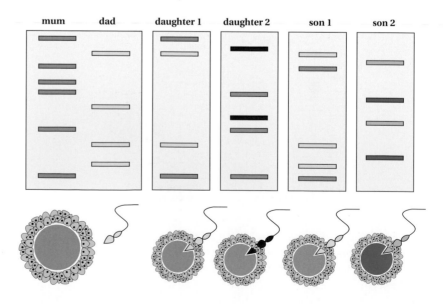

Fig 41
DNA profiles from one particular family. We inherit our DNA from our parents, and any bands that we do not get from our mother must come from our father. In this example, daughter 1 and son 1 clearly have their parents' DNA; daughter 2 is a step-daughter from mum's previous partner, while son 2 is adopted

How Science Works

In science, we make advances by a combination of two processes:

1 **Observation** – we look at the world and say 'Could it possibly be...?' and then come up with testable ideas. We call these *hypotheses*.

2 **Experimentation** – we gather evidence and analyse the data to draw reliable conclusions. Sometimes we gather support for our hypothesis, and sometimes we disprove it. Importantly, we never, ever, prove anything. So don't write this in your conclusions.

From your practical investigations in biology you will already be familiar with many of the basic principles used by scientists in their research. The rules that follow should be applied to any scientific investigation.

Testing a hypothesis

Fig H1 summarises the stages in scientific research.

Progress in science is made when a hypothesis is tested by an experiment. Contrary to popular belief, scientists do not just do experiments to see what happens. Fun though it might be, they don't just mix chemicals together and watch the results.

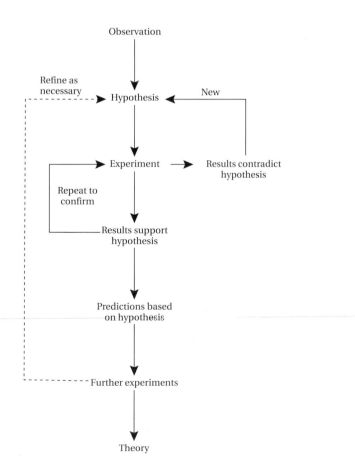

Fig H1
The stages of scientific research

An experiment must be designed to test one possible explanation of an observation. The definition of a good hypothesis is that an experiment can either support or disprove it. Strictly speaking, experiments can never prove that a hypothesis is absolutely, definitely correct. There is always the possibility that another explanation, one that no one has thought of, could fit the evidence equally well. However, an experiment can prove that a hypothesis is definitely wrong.

Unfortunately, people are often tempted to bypass the testing stage and go straight to an explanation without obtaining any experimental evidence. Some people seem to be uncomfortable when they are unable to find an explanation for a phenomenon. Even scientists have a tendency to be biased towards finding evidence to support their hypothesis.

As a student, you may well have done an investigation during which you were disappointed to get results that disproved your hypothesis. Or maybe your results were not what you expected. When this happens students often suggest that their experiment has 'gone wrong'; but, in scientific research, negative results are just as important as positive results.

When does a hypothesis become an accepted theory?

A hypothesis only becomes accepted theory when it has been thoroughly tested. The hypothesis may suggest predictions that, in turn, can be tested by further experiments and observations. Other scientists try to think of alternative interpretations of the results. It is normal practice for one scientist to be critical of another's published results. To ensure that published work is of sufficiently high quality, journals practise 'peer review' – a submitted paper is reviewed by two or three other experts in the field to make sure the experiments have been carried out well, and that the way the results have been interpreted is reasonable.

Essential Notes

The term 'expert in the field' is used to describe a scientist with experience and a great deal of knowledge in a particular area of science. In peer review, the scientists reviewing their colleagues' (peers') research, need to work in the same area of science, to be able to give a reliable and useful opinion of its quality.

It should also be possible to repeat an experiment and get the same results. Only after many confirmatory experiments is it likely that a new idea will be accepted. For example, for many years it was thought that cell membranes had a structure rather like a sandwich with protein 'bread' and phospholipid 'filling'. After many experiments this hypothesis was shown to be false, and it has now been replaced by the fluid-mosaic explanation described in this unit. This idea is now so well supported that it is described as the *theory of plasma membrane structure*.

Once a hypothesis is supported in this way – by many experimental results and observations – it may be accepted as the best explanation of an observation. A theory is, therefore, a well-established hypothesis that is supported by a substantial body of evidence. The theory of natural selection, for example, is based on huge numbers of observations, predictions and experiments that support the underlying hypothesis.

Designing an investigation

Suppose you are asked to design an experiment to investigate the effect of temperature on the rate of reaction of an enzyme such as catalase.

Your hypothesis could be:

Temperature has an effect on the rate of enzyme-controlled reactions.

Variables and controls

Catalase breaks down hydrogen peroxide to water and oxygen. To investigate the effect of temperature on the reaction, you could set up water baths at a range of temperatures, mix the catalase and hydrogen peroxide and measure the amount of oxygen released at each temperature.

There are, of course, practical difficulties to be overcome, such as collecting the oxygen without letting any escape, but in principle the experiment is quite simple. The key to this and all similar experiments is that you do three things:

- Select and set up a range of different values for the factor whose effect you are testing, in this case temperature. This is the *independent variable*.

- Measure the change in the factor that you are testing, in this case the rate of oxygen production. This is the *dependent variable*.

- Keep all other factors, such as enzyme and hydrogen peroxide concentrations, the same. These are the *controlled variables*.

Including a control experiment

One other precaution is to carry out a *control* experiment. This is not the same as keeping other variables constant. Its purpose is to ensure that changes made to the independent variable have not in themselves changed any other factor, and that the results really are due to the factor being tested.

For example, in the enzyme investigation featured above, how do we know that it is the enzyme that is breaking down the substrate and not simply the effect of temperature, or some other chemical in the enzyme solution? To answer this question, we must do a control experiment in which the enzyme is first boiled (to denature it), or left out altogether. If no oxygen is produced, we have shown that it really was the enzyme that was catalysing the reaction, not another factor.

Another example of a control can be taken from the common practical to test how effectively different antiseptics kill bacteria. Paper discs soaked in the antiseptic might be placed on a bacterial lawn in a Petri dish (see Fig H2).

In this experiment four of the discs were soaked in different antiseptics. The fifth disc was the control. The control disc should not be just a plain paper disc, but a disc that has also been soaked in sterile water, or whatever solvent was used in the antiseptics. This would show that the results obtained were really due to the antiseptics and not, perhaps, to something that could dissolve from the paper disc.

Examiners' Notes

- The *independent* variable is the one the experimenter changes. The *dependent* variable is the one the experimenter measures.

- All other possible variables are kept constant.

Fig H2
The effect of antiseptic discs on
bacteria growth

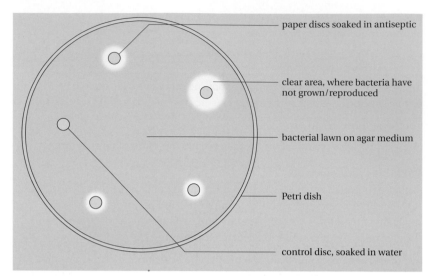

paper discs soaked in antiseptic

clear area, where bacteria have
not grown/reproduced

bacterial lawn on agar medium

Petri dish

control disc, soaked in water

What happens if it is not possible to control all the variables?

Sometimes it is not easy to ensure that all the major factors have been controlled. In an experiment on enzyme activity, controlling all the variables, apart from the independent variable you want to test, is quite straightforward. However, when experimenting with living organisms, investigations are rarely so simple because living things, themselves, are so variable.

If you are measuring the response of an animal to a stimulus, such as a woodlouse to light, you can never be sure that every single woodlouse will respond in the same way. Although most woodlice will move away from light, some might not. Even the simplest organisms respond to many stimuli. A living thing may behave untypically according to how well fed it is, its age, the time of day, its sexual maturity, or just because it is genetically different from most.

The only way to deal with this uncontrollable variability is to *repeat* an experiment several times and to use a large number of different organisms. Even in an experiment like the one using catalase it would be necessary to repeat the procedure several times for each value of the independent variable. For example, you would make several measurements of the rate of oxygen production at 35 °C, and several at 40 °C. Each repeat is called a *replicate*. Repetition increases the *reliability* of the results, and this increases the likelihood of being able to draw *valid* conclusions.

For students, there is nearly always a limit to the number of times an experiment can be repeated. Even researchers have time and resource constraints, and it is necessary to use judgement about the likely reliability of a set of data. If the results from replicates are all very similar, it is more likely that the results are reliable.

Accuracy and limitations

There is a limit to the accuracy of any measurement made in the course of an experiment. One limiting factor is the accuracy of the measuring instrument. A second is the care with which the instrument is used. But in biological experiments there is often a practical limit to the accuracy that it is worth trying to achieve. Although instruments exist which can measure length to a fraction of a micrometre, there would be no point in such accuracy when measuring tail length in mice in an investigation of variation. In fact, with a wriggling mouse, it might be difficult to measure even to the nearest millimetre. This difficulty would be compounded by having to decide exactly where the base of the tail actually starts. It is important, therefore, to consider the accuracy that might reasonably be expected from a set of data.

Accuracy is often confused with *reliability*. Consider the data in Table H1.

Leaf	Loss in mass over 24 hours/gram	
	Plant A	Plant B
1	1.03	0.28
2	0.96	0.72
3	0.89	0.74
4	1.05	0.69
5	0.94	0.64
Mean	0.968	0.64

Table H1
Comparing loss in mass of leaves from two different types of plants

Taking measurements from several specimens increases the reliability of the results, but it does not make them more accurate. For Plant A, all the results are reasonably similar, which suggests that the value for the mean is probably quite reliable. However, if another five leaves were measured, it is highly unlikely that exactly the same mean would be obtained.

The mean is given to three significant figures, but the results only to two significant figures. It is clearly absurd to give a value for the mean that is more precise than the accuracy of the measurements. Calculators give answers to many decimal places, but judgement has to be used about the number of significant figures that can sensibly be given in data for means, or other calculations that are derived by manipulating raw data.

The mean for Plant B looks unreliable. The result for Leaf 1 is very different from all of the others, so the mean comes well below all the other results. It may be that this result was a mistaken reading of the balance. On the other hand, the anomaly may have been because the leaf was atypical: it may have been much smaller, with fewer stomata than normal, or half-dead, for example. Without information about the original masses from which the losses were calculated it is impossible to guess. Expressing the results as a percentage loss rather than as total loss would make comparison more reasonable.

Associations and correlations: What affects what?

Many biological investigations depend on a combination of observation and data analysis rather than on actual experiments. This is because it is often not practical to carry out proper controlled experiments with living organisms in the field. There are two reasons for this:

- Logistical reasons – the complexity of interrelationships between organisms and the environment makes it virtually impossible.
- Ethical reasons – it is, for example, not ethical to remove the whole population of one species in an ecosystem in order to find the effect on the food web. Similarly you can't experiment on the effects of smoking by taking two groups of people and making one group smoke and the other group not, while keeping all other factors the same.

Investigators, therefore, have to look for associations that occur in the normal course of events. However, care needs to be taken when drawing conclusions. The number of fish in a lake affected by acid rain or some other pollutant may decline, but this does not necessarily mean that the pollution has caused the decline, or even that the two are connected. Further investigations could look for data on natural populations of particular fish species in water of different acidity. It would also be possible to carry out laboratory experiments to determine fish survival rates in water of different acidity. Results might well show that the lower the pH, the lower the survival rate. In this case there would be a correlation between pH and fish survival. This would still not prove that the decline in fish numbers in the lake was actually caused by the acidity.

If you counted, say, the number of nightclubs and pubs and the number of churches in several towns and cities and then plotted a graph of one against the other, you would almost certainly find a correlation. But this would obviously not prove that churches cause nightclubs and pubs to be built, or the other way round. The correlation is likely to be the result of a completely separate factor, probably the size of the town or city.

Similarly the decline in fish numbers might be due to some other factor, which might or might not be due to acidity. There could be an indirect association, caused by the effect of acidity on the food supply or the acid-related release of toxic mineral ions. A laboratory experiment would be unable to mimic the complex interaction of abiotic and biotic factors in the real situation of the lake.

Nevertheless, it is only by searching for correlations and investigating them further that biologists can increase their understanding of ecology.

Essential Notes

A correlation may be either positive or negative. When one factor increases as another increases it is a positive correlation; when one increases while another decreases it is a negative correlation.

Experiments on humans

This heading may bring to mind a Frankenstein-like image but, in fact, many experiments in biology are done with human subjects, to investigate the causes of particular diseases, and to test potential drugs and treatments.

Fig H3
A line graph is a simple way of showing a correlation between two variables. You should be able to look at a graph and describe it in one or two sentences.

a Positive correlation: as x increases, y increases

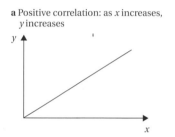

b Negative correlation: as x increases, y decreases

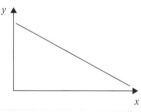

c As x increases, y increases up to a point, after which increasing x has no effect

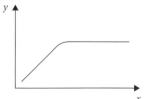

Studying human epidemiology

It is just as hard, if not harder, to use experiments to establish links between human diseases and factors such as environmental pollutants, diet, smoking and other aspects of lifestyle as it is to test, for example, the response of a woodlouse to light.

Most associations have been established by studying the incidence of disease or disorders in large groups of people. Looking for patterns in the occurrence of disease in human populations is called 'epidemiology'. Many of the suggested links have been controversial and some have caused considerable confusion in the minds of the public. There are still some people who refuse to accept the association between smoking and lung cancer, despite the overwhelming statistical evidence. The stages in establishing the cause of a non-infectious disease are:

- Look for a correlation between a disease and a specific factor.

- Develop hypotheses that could explain how the factor might have its effect.

- Test these hypotheses to find out whether the factor can cause the disease.

Establishing a correlation involves collecting data from large numbers of people. People and their lifestyles are hugely variable, so it is important to make comparisons between matched groups as far as possible. For example, suppose you were looking for a correlation between beer drinking and heart disease. It would not be enough just to compare the rates of heart disease between 1 000 beer drinkers and 1 000 non-beer drinkers. The ideal comparison would be between groups of people where the only difference in lifestyle was whether or not they drank beer.

In practice this would be virtually impossible to achieve. But, if groups were matched for age, sex, amount of exercise taken and major features of diet, the comparison would be much more valid.

It is very difficult to eliminate the possibility that any correlation is not due to some other linked factor. It may be, for example, that people who like drinking beer also like eating fish and chips, and eat them often. Or, they might have a genetic predisposition to heart disease. The latter is particularly difficult to argue against: those that challenge the evidence linking smoking to lung cancer often use it to put doubt in people's minds.

Once a correlation has been found, the next stage is try to determine how the factor actually causes its effect. This is often much more difficult. Many diseases, such as heart disease and cancers develop as a result of several factors that all interact. The correlation between smoking and incidence of lung cancer has been established for many years but no single specific carcinogen in cigarette smoke has yet been identified. The tar inhaled in cigarette smoke contains a massive cocktail of hundreds of organic compounds. Many of these may have carcinogenic properties, and may affect different people in different ways. Individuals differ in their susceptibility, probably due to genetic factors.

Research on the chemicals in tar, experiments on animals and with tissue cultures, and comparisons between many genetically distinct groupings of people have been done, but the only way to avoid the carcinogenic effects of smoking is never to smoke. One day, if a precise mechanism is discovered, it may be possible to produce non-harmful cigarettes, but this seems remote.

Human clinical trials to test new drugs

Drug testing is an area where good scientific practice is vital. When testing new drugs on human patients, it is not good enough to give some patients the new drug and give nothing to the control group. The patients in the control group should get a pill that is exactly the same as the one with the new drug except for the absence of the active ingredient. A pill without any active ingredient is called a 'placebo'.

Clinical trials usually involve *double-blind* investigations. The aim of these is to eliminate subjective bias on the part of both experimental subjects and the experimenters. In a double-blind experiment, neither the individuals nor the researchers know who belongs to the control group and the experimental group. Only after all the data has been obtained do the researchers learn which individuals are which. Performing an investigation in this way lessens the influence of psychological effects, such as prejudices and unintentional physical cues, on the results. Assignment of the subject to the experimental or control group must be done in a random way. The information that identifies the subjects and which group they belonged to is kept by a third party and not given to the researchers until the study is over. Double-blind methods should be applied to any trial where there is the possibility that the results will be affected by conscious or unconscious bias on the part of the experimenter.

Normally, drug trials take place in three phases:

- **A Phase I trial** – is an early stage clinical trial in which an experimental drug is tested in a small number of healthy human volunteers to check if it is safe; i.e. there are no side-effects. This type of trial does not test whether a drug works against a particular disease.

- **A Phase II trial** – is the next stage clinical trial in which an experimental drug that has successfully passed through a Phase I trial is tested to see if it can treat a specific disease or condition. Human volunteers with the disease or condition are given either the experimental drug or a standard drug, as a control. The groups are then compared to see which drug is the most beneficial.

- **A Phase III trial** – has a similar format to a Phase II trial but involves a larger number of human patients – usually hundreds or thousands. A drug must pass successfully through Phase III trials before it can be approved for general use.

Practice exam-style questions

1 A group of students were given some maggots that are always found in dark environments. They were given two alternative explanations.

Alternative 1: The maggots are moving directly from the direction of the light source in a straight line towards the dark.

Alternative 2: They are crawling around in random directions, making turns until they happen to reach the preferred half, where they remain.

(a) What type of response is being described in each of these alternatives?

_____

_____ 2 marks

(b) Explain how you would set about finding out which alternative is the more likely explanation.

_____

_____

_____

_____ 4 marks

Total marks: 6

2 The graph (Fig E1) shows the distribution of rods and cones in the human retina.

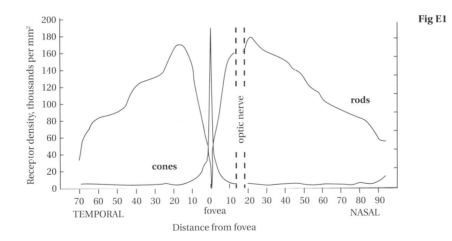

Fig E1

(a) Describe the distribution of rods and cones across the retina.

_____

_____

_____ 3 marks

(b) What is the total receptor density at 50 units from the fovea on the temporal side?

_____ 1 mark

(c) Use the graph to explain why we can still distinguish the colour of an object when viewed out of the corner of the eye.

_____ 1 mark

(d) There is little difference in the peak density of rods and cones. Explain why visual acuity is much greater with the cones.

_____

_____ 2 marks

Total marks: 7

3   The diagram (Fig E2) shows a reflex arc.

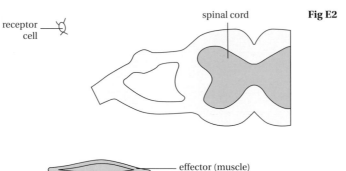

receptor cell

spinal cord   **Fig E2**

effector (muscle)

(a) Complete the diagram of a reflex arc by drawing and labelling the sensory neurone, relay neurone and motor neurone.

_____

_____

_____ 3 marks

(b) List three features of reflex arcs.

_____

_____

_____ 3 marks

(c) Explain how the structure of a synapse prevents impulses being passed in both directions.

_____

_____ 2 marks

Total marks: 8

4   A single Pacinian corpuscle (pressure receptor) in the skin was isolated and stimulated with a period of light pressure followed by a period of heavier pressure (Fig E3). The trace shows the action potentials that passed down the sensory neurone.

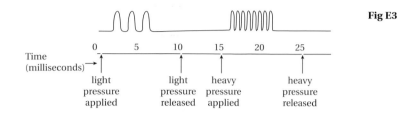

Fig E3

(a)   Explain how the trace illustrates the '**all or nothing**' principle.

_____

_____ 2 marks

(b)   Use the diagram to explain how the body distinguishes between stimuli of different intensities.

_____ 1 mark

(c)   **(i)**   Explain why the impulses stop before the stimulus ends.

_____

_____ 2 marks

(ii)   Suggest the advantage of this property.

_____

_____ 2 marks

Total marks: 7

5   Steps (i) to (viii) are events that occur in synaptic transmission.

(i)   Calcium ions activate vesicles.

(ii)   Transmitter diffuses across synaptic cleft.

(iii)   EPSP builds up.

(iv)   Calcium ions diffuse into synaptic knob.

(v)   Threshold is reached.

(vi)   Action potential arrives at synaptic knob.

(vii) Sodium ions diffuse into postsynaptic cleft.

(viii) Transmitter fits into receptors on postsynaptic membrane.

(a)   List the events in the correct order.

_____

_____ 2 marks

(b) Explain why the presence of mitochondria is essential at the synaptic knob.

_____

_____

_____ 3 marks

The krait is a venomous snake whose bite contains a powerful neurotoxin called bungarotoxin. The toxin blocks the acetylcholine receptor sites on neuromuscular junctions.

(c) Explain what effect bungarotoxin will have on anyone who is bitten.

_____

_____ 2 marks

Total marks: 7

6   The diagram (Fig E4) shows the banding pattern in one sarcomere of skeletal muscle.

Relaxed sarcomere   **Fig E4**

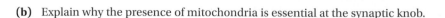

(a) Draw or describe the sarcomere as it would appear when contracted.

_____

_____ 2 marks

(b) Outline the role of calcium ions in muscular contraction.

_____

_____

_____ 3 marks

The muscle fibre types of a selection of age-matched athletes were analysed, and the results are summarised in the table below. These are average values; there is considerable variation between athletes.

Type of athlete	Approx. % fast-twitch	Approx. % slow-twitch
Marathon runner	18	82
Swimmer	25	75
Cyclist	40	60
800-metre runner	52	48
Untrained person	55	45
Sprinter and jumper	62	38

Analysis of the average proportions of male athletes

(c) What does 'age-matched' mean? Explain why age matching is important.

_____

_____ 2 marks

(d) Explain in general terms how the proportion of fast- and slow-twitch fibres is related to the nature of an athlete's chosen activity.

_____

_____ 2 marks

(e) What statistical test could you apply to the results to see if they were statistically significant? Explain your choice.

_____

_____

_____ 3 marks

(f) In which type of muscle fibre would you expect to find the highest density of mitochondria? Explain your answer.

_____

_____ 2 marks

Total marks: 14

7 (a) Explain why athletes generate heat when they run.

_____

_____ 2 marks

(b) Explain how the body responds to a rise in core temperature.

_____

_____

_____

_____ 4 marks

(c) Explain why overheating is more of a problem in humid conditions than in dry conditions.

_____

_____ 2 marks

Total marks: 8

8

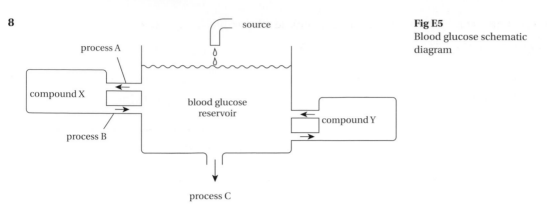

Fig E5
Blood glucose schematic
diagram

(a) Compound X (Fig E5) is a carbohydrate, compound Y is not. Name both compounds.

_____

_____ 2 marks

(b) Name the main source of blood glucose.

_____ 1 mark

(c) Name the processes A, B and C.

_____

_____

_____ 3 marks

(d) Which process would be stimulated by insulin?

_____ 1 mark

(e) Which process would be stimulated by glucagon?

_____ 1 mark

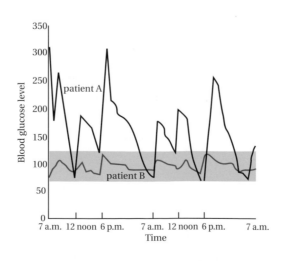

Fig E6

The graph (Fig E6) shows the blood glucose levels of two individuals over a two-day period.

(f) Suggest what is represented by the yellow shaded area.

_____ 1 mark

(g) Identify which patient is the diabetic. Explain your choice.

_____ 1 mark

(h) Describe how the body detects and responds to a rise in blood glucose levels.

_____

_____

_____

_____

_____ 5 marks

Total marks: 15

9 (a) Explain the difference between a positive and a negative feedback.

_____

_____ 2 marks

Testosterone is the main sex steroid in males. The flow diagram (Fig E7) illustrates the control of testosterone.

(b) Explain how a negative feedback system operates to keep the levels of testosterone constant.

_____

_____

_____ 3 marks

hypothalamus ◄ ─ ─ ╮   **Fig E7**

gonadotrophin releasing hormone (GnRH)
(via local capillaries)

anterior pituitary

luteinising hormone (LH)
(via circulating blood)

testes

testosterone ─ ─ ╯

LH (Fig E7) is a hormone also found in females, where it has a different function.

(c) Explain how the same hormone can have different effects on males and females.

_____

_____ 2 marks

(d) Outline the mode of action of steroid hormones.

_____

_____

_____ 3 marks

Total marks: 10

10 Sickle cell anaemia is a genetic disease. Sufferers have an abnormal form of haemoglobin. Analysis of DNA has shown that it is caused by a mutation on the gene for the beta chain of haemoglobin. The table below contains the base sequence of a healthy individual.

(a) Fill in the missing codons in the grid below.

Codon	4	5	6
DNA	ACT		
mRNA		GGA	
tRNA			GAG
Amino acid	Threonine	Proline	Glutamic acid

3 marks

Sickle cell anaemia is caused by a mutation to codon 6, in which GAG is changed to GTG, which codes for the amino acid valine.

(b) What is the name given to this type of gene mutation?

_____ 1 mark

(c) Explain how such a tiny change can have a potentially lethal effect on the people who inherit the disease.

_____

_____

_____ 3 marks

Total marks: 7

11 A short piece of mRNA reads:

CUUCAAGCGAAC

(a) What would be the complementary DNA sequence?

_____ 1 mark

(b) What is the name given to a piece of DNA made using mRNA as a template?

_____ 1 mark

(c) What is the name of the enzyme that can carry out this process?

_____ 1 mark

(d) Suggest one reason why scientists would want to make a piece of DNA from mRNA.

_____ 1 mark

(e) Give two similarities and two differences between the structures of mRNA and tRNA.

_____

_____

_____

_____ 4 marks

Total marks: 8

12 One line of stem cell research is focusing on creating new skin to help burn victims and people with diabetic skin ulcers. Stem cells are seeded onto a synthetic scaffold before being transferred to the wound. It is hoped that this new treatment will avoid the need for skin grafts.

(a) Explain what is meant by stem cell.

_____

_____ 2 marks

(b) Explain how a stem cell becomes specialised to form a skin cell.

_____

_____ 2 marks

(c) Explain why the new treatment is preferable to skin grafts.

_____

_____ 2 marks

(d) Give two possible objections to the use of stem cells in medicine.

_____

_____ 2 marks

Total marks: 8

13 The disease GSD 1a (glycogen storage disease type 1a) results from a recessive allele that fails to make the enzyme glucose-6-phosphatase. As a result, individuals cannot break down glycogen when required. At present there is no cure, and sufferers have to eat large amounts of starch.

(a) Explain how a healthy individual responds to a fall in blood glucose levels (details of hormone action not required).

_____

_____

_____ 3 marks

(b) Explain why heterozygotes do not suffer from the disease GSD 1a.

_____

_____ 2 marks

(c) Explain why sufferers from GSD 1a have to eat large amounts of starch.

_____

_____ 2 marks

Some recent research has focused on the possibility of treating GSD 1a with gene therapy. Working copies of the glucose-6-oxidase gene are put into viruses that will transfer the gene into liver cells.

(d) Explain why viruses are suitable vectors in gene therapy.

_____

_____ 2 marks

(e) Suggest two possible problems with this type of gene therapy.

_____

_____ 2 marks

(f) Outline the trials that will have to be completed before this type of treatment becomes widely available. (This is from 'How Science Works', as covered at AS level.)

_____

_____

_____ 3 marks

Total marks: 14

Answers

Question	Answer	Marks
1 (a)	Alternative 1 = taxis (if maggots consistently move to dark with few turns). Alternative 2 = kinesis (if maggots make many more turns).	2
1 (b)	*Any four from*: Use choice chamber. Separate light from dark. Use batch of identical maggots/same species/age. Take one maggot. Count number of turns. Measure time taken to find dark. Repeat.	4
		Total 6
2 (a)	*Any three from*: Rods are concentrated away from the fovea. Cones are concentrated at the fovea. There are a small number of cones across the retina. There are more rods than cones in total.	3
2 (b)	$84\,000/mm^2$ (accept 82–86); 80 000 rods plus about 4 000 cones	1
2 (c)	Cones are found over all of the retina.	1
2 (d)	*Any two from*: Retinal convergence is greater in the cones (or vice-versa). There is more information per unit area from the cones than from the rods. There are more neurones per cone in the optic nerve.	2
		Total 7
3 (a)		3, 1 mark for each neurone in position and correctly labelled
3 (b)	*Any three from*: Reflex arcs have few neurones. They are rapid. They are fixed (one stimulus = one response). They are not under conscious control.	3

Question	Answer	Marks
3 (c)	The transmitter only is made at the presynaptic membrane. The receptors/receptor proteins only are on the postsynaptic membrane.	2
		Total 8
4 (a)	*Any two from*: All impulses are the same height/size/amplitude. Whatever the size of the stimulus, they are the same. There are no big or small impulses.	2
4 (b)	The more intense the stimulus, the greater the frequency of impulses.	1
4 (c) (i)	*Any two from*: The receptor has adapted. Gel in the Pacinian corpuscle absorbs pressure. The receptor cells not deformed/resumes normal shape.	2
4 (c) (ii)	CNS is not overloaded with irrelevant/old information. This allows the individual to focus on new information.	2
		Total 7
5 (a)	1 = (vi), 2 = (iv), 3 = (i), 4 = (ii), 5 = (viii), 6 = (vii), 7 = (iii), 8 = (v)	2
5 (b)	Mitochondria produce energy required for: re-synthesis of transmitter substance active transport of calcium ions out of synaptic knob.	3
5 (c)	Bungarotoxin will cause paralysis/muscles cannot contract. This is because acetylcholine cannot fit into receptors. There is no ion movement/no depolarisation.	2
		Total 7
6 (a)	Contracted sarcomere Vital points: sarcomere is short; dark bands are wide.	2, 1 mark for each
6 (b)	Calcium diffuses into the muscle fibre across sarcoplasmic reticulum. Binds to/activates troponin. Active troponin moves tropomyosin (so that actin can bind to myosin).	3
6 (c)	*Any two from*: 'Age-matched' means that the men in the sample were of similar age. A control is an important variable. It makes comparison valid.	2
6 (d)	Longer events/stamina events require slow-twitch fibres. Short/power events require fast-twitch fibres.	2

Question	Answer	Marks
6 (e)	Chi squared is the statistical test to apply to the results. This test is used to see if there was a *significant* difference between the observed results and those you would expect by chance/if there was no correlation.	3
6 (f)	There are more mitochondria in slow-twitch fibres. This is because they get the most ATP from *aerobic* respiration.	2
		Total 14
7 (a)	*Any two from*: Movement of muscles creates heat. Energy transfers are inefficient. The transfer of energy from glucose to ATP in respiration generates heat. Running causes transfer of energy from ATP to actin/myosin.	2
7 (b)	*Any four from*: There is a rise in blood temperature which is detected by the *hypothalamus*. The heat loss centre ... ... initiates impulses. Sweating – energy lost as water evaporates (*'sweating' on its own = 0 marks*). Latent heat of evaporation. Vasodilation – arterioles widen, greater blood flow to surface capillaries. Decrease in metabolic rate Lowering hairs	4 (**NB**: marks awarded for A-level detail, not GCSE level)
7 (c)	In humid conditions there is less of a water potential gradient (*or vice-versa*). Evaporation is slower.	2
		Total 8
8 (a)	X = glycogen Y = lipid/triglyceride	2, 1 for each
8 (b)	The main source of blood glucose is from digestion/absorption of carbohydrate.	1
8 (c)	A = glycogenesis B – glycogenolysis C = respiration	3, 1 for each
8 (d)	Process B is stimulated by glucagon.	1
8 (e)	Process A is stimulated by insulin.	1
8 (f)	It represents normal range of blood glucose levels (*accept: no symptoms*).	1
8 (g)	Patient A; he or she cannot control blood glucose within normal limits.	1
8 (h)	*Any five from*: Rise is detected by the β cells. The β cells secrete insulin. Insulin travels in blood. Target cells are affected, mainly in the liver. Insulin fits into specific protein receptors. This stimulates extra glucose channels to open.	

Question	Answer	Marks
	Glucose leaves the blood and enters the cells. Insulin activates enzyme pathways. These pathways metabolise glucose.	5
		Total 15
9 (a)	Negative feedback is a mechanism that keeps conditions constant. Positive feedback is a mechanism that brings about further change.	2
9 (b)	Too much testosterone is detected by the hypothalamus. Therefore less GnRH is made. So less LH is made and less testosterone is made/secreted. (*NB: converse approach also acceptable – too little testosterone …*)	3
9 (c)	*Any two from*: Males and females have different membrane receptor proteins. There is a different pathway of second messengers in the cytoplasm. Different enzymes are activated/deactivated.	2
9 (d)	*Any three from*: Hormone passes through cell membrane. It binds to nuclear/intracellular receptors. Transcription factors are activated. Specific genes are expressed/transcribed.	3
		Total 10
10 (a)	<table><tr><td>Codon</td><td>4</td><td>5</td><td>6</td></tr><tr><td>DNA</td><td>ACT</td><td>CCT</td><td>GAG</td></tr><tr><td>mRNA</td><td>UGA</td><td>GGA</td><td>CUC</td></tr><tr><td>tRNA</td><td>ACU</td><td>CCU</td><td>GAG</td></tr><tr><td>Amino acid</td><td>Threonine</td><td>Proline</td><td>Glutamic acid</td></tr></table>	3, 1 per correct column
10 (b)	This type of mutation is a substitution or point mutation.	1
10 (c)	*Any three from*: different base sequence; different amino acid sequence/primary structure of protein; folds and bends; into different tertiary structure; protein/haemoglobin a different shape, so won't function as normal.	3
		Total 7
11 (a)	GAAGTTCGCTTG	1
11 (b)	cDNA	1
11 (c)	Reverse transcriptase is the enzyme that can carry out this process.	1
11 (d)	Scientists would want to make a piece of DNA from mRNA to find a gene/clone a gene/for PCR/use in gene therapy.	1
11 (e)	Similarities: same four nucleotides/bases/CTAU; single stranded. Differences: tRNA folded, mRNA not; 64 different types of tRNA, thousands of mRNAs; mRNA not involved in transcription.	4
		Total 8

Question	Answer	Marks
12 (a)	A stem cell is an undifferentiated cell that has the potential to develop into other specialised cell types.	2
12 (b)	Specialisation is caused by the selective activation of genes. Particular genes are transcribed/expressed. This happens when all necessary transcription factors are in place.	2
12 (c)	Taking skin from another part of the body is painful. Reference to healing time for that part of body/infection risk.	2
12 (d)	If embryonic stem cells are to be used, there could be ethical objections to the use of an embryo. Another objection could be the possible introduction of harmful viruses.	2
		Total 8
13 (a)	It would be detected by α cells in islets of Langerhans which secrete glucagon. Glucagon activates enzymes/glucose-6-phosphatase. This stimulates breakdown of glycogen.	3
13 (b)	Heterozygotes possess one healthy allele. One healthy allele is all they need to make the working enzyme.	2
13 (c)	The digestion/hydrolysis of starch … … releases glucose slowly into the blood preventing glucose levels falling too low.	2
13 (d)	Viruses can be made to target specific cells. Thus deliver DNA/genes/genetic material directly into the cell.	2
13 (e)	*Any two from*: It is not possible to be absolutely certain what the virus will do in the body. It could enter cells other than the liver. It could cause disease. Immune reactions to the altered virus might cause problems.	2
13 (f)	*Any three from*: After animal studies have shown that the gene therapy works in principle … … it needs to be thoroughly tested in humans … Test using the standard methods of Phase I, Phase II and Phase III clinical trials. It would be unethical to test gene therapy in healthy volunteers – so all trials would need to be done in people with the disease. In the case of a rare disease, it is often difficult to get enough data to show that gene therapy is safe and that it works.	3
		Total 14

Glossary

Acetylcholine (Ach)	Transmitter substance secreted from the synapses of many nerves, including most of the peripheral nervous system, and the parasympathetic nervous system (*PSNS*).
Acetylcholinesterase	Enzyme found in the synaptic cleft of cholinergic nerves, where it breaks down acetylcholine, preventing over-stimulation.
Actin	Protein involved in muscular contraction. See also *myosin*.
Action potential	A nerve impulse, a wave of depolarisation that spreads along the axon.
Addition	Type of gene mutation in which a base is added, causing a frame shift in one direction, so that many codons are changed. See also *deletion*, *substitution*, *mutation*.
Adenyl cyclase	Vital enzyme in mechanism of hormone action. Basic sequence of events: Hormone fits into receptor on cell surface membrane → adenyl cyclase activated → second messenger activated → enzymes in cell activated or deactivated.
Adrenaline	Fast-acting hormone, secreted by the adrenal glands, that prepares the body for action. Effects include raised heart beat, blood pressure and blood glucose levels.
Adrenergic synapse	In the sympathetic nervous system (*SNS*); synapse that secretes noradrenaline.
All or nothing	All nerve impulses are of the same amplitude. If a stimulus reaches a threshold, an impulse is generated. If not, there is no impulse. There are no big or small impulses.
Anticodon	Sequence of three bases found on a *transfer RNA* molecule, that codes for a specific amino acid. An anticodon binds to a complementary codon on messenger RNA (mRNA) during translation.
Auxin	A plant growth regulator. Often called a plant hormone.
Basal metabolic rate (BMR)	Measured as oxygen consumption per unit body mass per unit time, when organism is at rest.
Blind spot	Point on the retina where the optic nerve joins. Has no rods or cones so nothing is perceived in that area.
Carcinogen	Cancer-causing agent. Basically the same as a *mutagen*.
Cardiovascular centre	Region of the brain responsible for initiating the impulses that modify heart rate. Situated in the medulla oblongata of the hindbrain.
Cholinergic synapse	Synapse that secretes acetylcholine (Ach).
Cloning	Process of making a genetically identical copy. Can apply to a piece of DNA, a gene, cell, tissue or whole organism.
Codon	A group of three bases in DNA or RNA that codes for a particular amino acid. Also called a *triplet*.
Complementary DNA (cDNA)	Which has been made from mature RNA by reverse transcription. Unsurprisingly, catalysed by the enzyme reverse transcriptase.
Cyclic AMP	Second messenger in hormone action. When a hormone fits into a receptor site on the cell membrane, the enzyme *adenyl cyclase* is activated, turning ATP into cyclic AMP.

Cystic fibrosis	Recessive genetic disease in which a faulty allele fails to make a vital membrane protein (CFTR). The main symptom is a build up of sticky mucus in the lungs, pancreas and reproductive system.
Degenerate code	There are 64 different codons, but only 20 different amino acids, so some amino acids have several different codons.
Deletion	Type of gene mutation in which a base is lost (deleted). This causes a *frame shift*.
Dideoxy sequencing	Technique used to find the base sequence of a piece of DNA.
DNA polymerase	Enzyme that catalyses the addition of complementary nucleotides during DNA replication.
Ectotherm	An animal whose core body temperature is similar to that of the environment. Ectotherms can thermoregulate, but usually only by modifying their behaviour. Reptiles and amphibians are examples of ectotherms.
Endotherm	An animal that can maintain a stable core body temperature despite the environmental temperature. Mammals and birds are endotherms.
EPSP	Excitatory postsynaptic potential – a charge that builds up in a neurone after synaptic transmission. If the EPSP reaches a threshold, an impulse is created.
Fovea	Region of the retina where cones are concentrated, allowing us to see in detail and in colour.
Frame shift	In mutation, a situation where a base is added or lost, causing all other bases to move along one place in a particular direction.
FSH	Follicle stimulating hormone.
Glucagon	Hormone, secreted by the α cells in the *islets of Langerhans* of the pancreas, in response to low blood glucose levels. Antagonistic hormone to insulin.
Gluconeogenesis	The production of new glucose from non-carbohydrate sources (i.e. protein or lipid, but not glycogen). This happens during fasting/dieting/starvation, when glucose and glycogen levels are low.
Glycogen	The main storage carbohydrate in animals. A highly branched polymer of glucose, so it can be built up and broken down quickly. Stored in many cells, but notably those of the liver and muscles.
Glycogenesis	The production of glycogen by the polymerisation of glucose.
Glycogenolysis	The breakdown of glycogen to release glucose. Stimulated (indirectly) by the hormone glucagon.
Haemophilia	Genetic disease caused by a faulty allele that fails to make a vital blood-clotting protein. The most common type of haemophilia is sex linked (on X chromosome) and is caused by an inability to make Factor VIII.
Homeostasis	The ability of an organism to maintain its internal conditions within certain limits, for example, pH of blood, body temperature and blood glucose levels.
Hormone	Chemical, secreted by an endocrine gland, that has an effect on a target organ or cell.
Hypothalamus	Vital part of brain. Sensitive to many different internal and external stimuli. Controls the secretions of the pituitary gland and therefore of the whole endocrine system.
In vitro	'In glass' – processes carried out in test tubes, etc.
In vivo	'In life' – processes happening in living cells/tissues or whole organisms.

Insulin	Hormone made by β cells in *islets of Langerhans*. Works by stimulating cells to open extra glucose channels in cell membranes, so that glucose can leave the blood and enter cells, where it can be metabolised.
Iodopsin	Light-sensitive pigment found only in the cone cells on the *retina*.
IPSP	Inhibitory postsynaptic potential; a charge that builds up in the postsynaptic membrane of inhibitory synapses. IPSPs exist to inhibit action potential in particular neurones. See *EPSP*.
Islets of Langerhans	Patches of endocrine (hormone-producing) tissue in the pancreas. Contain α and β cells that secrete *glucagon* and *insulin*, respectively.
Kinesis	Simple behavioural response in animals, in which a stimulus leads to a non-directional response; for example, woodlice responding to light. See also *taxis*.
LH	Luteinising hormone. A gonadotrophin hormone secreted by the pituitary that triggers ovulation.
Ligase	Enzyme that joins together complementary sticky ends of DNA. Used in conjunction with restriction enzymes.
Messenger RNA (mRNA)	A single strand of nucleotides that is made on a gene during *transcription*. Basically, it is a mobile copy of a gene.
Motor neurone	A neurone that carries impulses from the CNS to an effector (muscle or gland).
Multipotent	Multipotent stem cells have limited potential, and can only differentiate into a few closely related cell types.
Mutagen	An environmental factor that causes mutation, such as ionising radiation, ultraviolet light and chemicals such as mustard gas and cigarette smoke.
Mutation	A change in an organism's DNA. Gene mutations are changes in the base sequence of a particular gene, while chromosome mutations involve changes in whole blocks of genes.
Myogenic	Originating from the muscle. Refers to the fact that cardiac muscle cells, and therefore the heart as a whole, beats on its own rather than needing nervous stimulation.
Myosin	Protein involved in muscular contraction. See *actin*.
Negative feedback	A control system for stability. A change is detected and initiates a corrective mechanism to reverse the change. Contrast with *positive feedback*.
Neuromuscular junction	Specialised synapse at the end of motor nerves, where they join muscle fibres.
Neurone	A specialised nerve cell that can transmit impulses.
Noradrenaline	Neurotransmitter released from the ends of sympathetic nerves.
Oestrogen	Female sex hormone. A steroid hormone, made in the ovaries, which has a vital role in the menstrual cycle. Promotes the development of female secondary sex characteristics, such as breasts, and also involved in the thickening of the endometrium following menstruation.
Oncogene	A protein-encoding gene which participates in the onset of cancer when it is deregulated.
Oocyte	An egg cell, or ovum.

Pacinian corpuscle	Touch receptor in the skin. Detects heavy pressure and vibration.
Palindromic sequence	A section of DNA where the sequence of bases on one strand reads the same as the sequence on the complementary strand when read from the other direction. For example, CGTACG will read GCATGC on the complementary strand, which is CGTACG when read from the other direction.
Parasympathetic nervous system (PSNS)	One division of the autonomic nervous system. Generally, stimulation of parasympathetic nerves will return the body to normal, for example, slowing down the heart. See also *sympathetic nervous system* (*SNS*).
PCR	Polymerase chain reaction – a method of cloning DNA in a test tube. This process requires an original sample of DNA, nucleotides, primers and the enzyme DNA polymerase.
Phenylketonuria (PKU)	A genetic disease in which a faulty allele fails to make the enzyme phenylalanine hydroxylase, so that the individual cannot convert phenylalanine to tyrosine. The result is a build up of the phenylalanine which leads to brain damage.
Pluripotent	Type of stem cell that can differentiate into a wide variety of the 216 different cell types. Has some potential in gene therapy.
Positive feedback	A control mechanism in which change leads to more change.
Progesterone	Female sex hormone. Progesterone is the hormone of pregnancy, secreted during the second half of the menstrual cycle and during the whole of pregnancy.
Proto-oncogenes	Proto-oncogenes code for proteins that aid the regulation of differentiation and cell growth. (A normal gene that can become an oncogene from mutations or increased gene expression.)
Receptor	A cell that can detect a particular *stimulus*. Receptors are able to transduce the energy in the stimulus into a nervous impulse.
Recognition site	Sequence of bases on a DNA molecule that is cut by a restriction enzyme, producing sticky ends. Recognition sites are usually palindromic, i.e. the sequence on opposing strands is the same, such as CTATAG, whose *palindromic sequence* is GATATC.
Reflex	Simple coordinated response that is generally fixed. One stimulus leads to a particular response.
Reflex arc	The pathway taken by impulses in a reflex. Generally involves very few neurones; sensory neurones, *relay neurones* (in the CNS) and motor neurones.
Refractory period	'Recovery period'. The time after a nerve impulse has passed when it is impossible (absolute refractory period) or more difficult (relative refractory period) to generate another impulse. Ensures that impulses are discrete, i.e. do not blend.
Relay neurone	Neurone in the spinal cord that directly connects sensory and motor neurones, thus completing the fastest possible circuit in a *reflex arc*.
Resting potential	A state of readiness in neurones. An electrical charge across the axon membrane, created by an unequal distribution of ions, where the outside is positive relative to the inside. See also *action potential*.
Restriction endonuclease	Enzyme that cuts DNA at specific recognition sites, to produce *sticky ends*.
Retina	Layer on the back of the eye that contains the rods and cones; photosensitive receptors.

Retinal convergence	Arrangement of neurones in the retina. Many rod cells converge into one sensory neurone in the optic nerve. There is much less convergence from the cone cells. Thus rods are more sensitive because they summate, but cones supply more detail per unit area of retina, resulting in much higher visual acuity.
Reverse transcriptase	Enzyme that makes DNA from RNA: *transcription* in reverse, hence the name.
Rhodopsin	Light-sensitive pigment found in rod cells. Made from retinine (made from vitamin A) and opsin, a protein.
Ribosome	Organelle that is the site of *translation* in protein synthesis. In eukaryotic cells, found free in the cytoplasm or attached to rough endoplasmic reticulum.
RNA polymerase	Enzyme that catalyses the addition of complementary nucleotides during transcription. The first stage of protein synthesis where the messenger RNA (mRNA) is assembled on a gene.
Saltatory conduction	Type of rapid conduction seen in myelinated nerves, where the impulse 'jumps' from node (of Ranvier) to node.
Sarcomere	In skeletal muscle, one repeated pattern of actin and myosin fibres. When actin and myosin slide over each other, the sarcomeres shorten and the muscle contracts.
Sarcoplasmic reticulum	Modified endoplasmic reticulum seen in muscle fibres. Motor impulses spread from neuromuscular junction along the sarcoplasmic reticulum, altering the permeability of the membrane to calcium. The influx of calcium initiates contraction.
Sensory neurone	Neurones that pass from receptors to the CNS, bringing sensory information about the internal and external environment.
Sickle cell anaemia	Genetic disease in which a faulty allele codes for haemoglobin that polymerises in areas of low oxygen concentration. This causes red cells to become sickle (banana) shaped. Sickle cells are not flexible and will cause blockages in capillary beds, leaving areas of tissue starved of oxygen.
Sino-atrial node (SAN)	The heart's pacemaker. Situated in the wall of the left atrium, the SAN generates the impulse that stimulates the atria and, after a delay, the ventricles, to contract.
Small interfering RNA (siRNA)	Small RNA molecules that can block transcription. Have potential in medicine to block harmful genes.
Stem cell	Undifferentiated cell that has the potential to develop/specialise into any other cell type. Has great potential in medicine.
Sticky ends	Staggered cuts in DNA, so that one strand is several bases longer than the other. Made by restriction enzymes.
Stimulus	A change in the environment that can be detected by a *receptor*.
Substitution	Type of mutation in which a particular base is replaced by a different base. Also known as a point mutation. Changes one codon, and one amino acid, but still has the potential to change the whole protein. Contrast with *addition* and *deletion*.
Sympathetic nervous system (SNS)	Part of the autonomic nervous system, along with the *parasympathetic nervous system* (*PSNS*).
Synapse	A junction between two neurones. Synapses allow the selection of different neural pathways – the underlying process behind all movement, thought and coordination.

Taq polymerase	Thermostable polymerase enzyme from the bacterium *Thermus aquatalis*. Used extensively in PCR because it is not denatured at the high temperatures needed.
Taxis	Simple behavioural response in which an organism moves towards or away from a directional stimulus. See also *kinesis*.
Totipotent	Type of stem cell, found in the embryo, that is totally potent; i.e. has the ability to develop into any cell type.
Transcription	First stage (of two) in protein synthesis. The base sequence on a particular gene is copied onto a molecule of *messenger RNA* (*mRNA*). Takes place in the nucleus.
Transfer RNA (tRNA)	A clover-leaf shaped molecule formed from a single strand of nucleotides that has an *anticodon* on one end and an amino acid binding site at the other.
Translation	Second stage (of two) in protein synthesis. The base sequence on the messenger RNA (mRNA) molecule is used to assemble a protein. Takes place on *ribosomes*.
Transmitter substance	Substance secreted by synapses. Transmitters such as *acetylcholine* (*Ach*) are released from vesicles in the presynaptic membrane.
Triplet	Group of three bases. Used interchangeably with the word *codon*. A sequence of three bases (for example, AAT, CGC) that codes for a particular amino acid.
Tropism	A growth response seen in plants. A negative phototropism is growth away from light, while a positive geotropism would be growth towards gravity.
Tropomyosin	Protein involved in muscular contraction. A long, thin, spiral protein that winds around actin, covering the myosin binding sites.
Troponin	Protein involved in muscular contraction. Troponin is activated by calcium ions. When activated, it binds to tropomyosin, moving it out of the way and allowing myosin to bind to actin.
Vasoconstriction	Narrowing of arterioles to reduce blood flow to a particular area/tissue, for example, to the skin when we are too cold.
Vasodilation	Widening of arterioles to increase blood flow to a particular area, for example, to the skin when we are too hot.
Vectors	Carriers. In genetic engineering, vectors carry genes or pieces of DNA from one cell to another. Liposomes and viruses are commonly used as vectors.
Visual acuity	The ability to see in detail. Acuteness or clarity of vision.

Index